PROSPECT OF COMPANY GROWTH AND FORECASTS MANAGEMENT

VAHID BIGLARI

Title: **Prospect of Company Growth and Forecasts Management**

Author: **Vahid Biglari**

Publisher: **Supreme Century**, Reseda, CA, USA

ISBN: **978-1939123473**

Library of Congress Control Number: **2018964670**

To my beloved wife, and my dearest parents

ABSTRACT

The opportunistic and efficiency views of the forecasts undertaken by managers are completely different. In the efficiency approach, it is believed that by providing accurate forecasts, management provides correct information to the market, thereby restricting them to do earnings management. Therefore forecasts are truthful. In contrast, the opportunistic view of forecasts is that management's forecasts consist of biased signals. Managers will use earnings and Forecasts Management (FM) as tools to create positive earnings surprises that will lead to temporary stock price appreciation or preventing stock price depreciation.

This research shows that as indicated by the companies' growth capabilities the Analysts' Recommendations (AR) can explain the difference in behaviours of managers under these two views. This research highlights the managers' decision in reporting pessimistic forecast to produce positive Forecasts Errors (FEs) when a company's shares are recommended to sell (hereafter called *sell companies*), and generate optimistic forecast when a company's shares are recommended to buy (hereafter called *buy companies*).

Previous researches show that *buy* (growth) companies conduct income increasing earnings management in order to meet forecasts and generate positive forecast Errors (FEs). This behavior however, is not inherent in *sell* (non-growth) companies. By referring to the existing framework in the literature, this research hypothesizes that since sell companies are pressured to avoid income increasing earnings management, they are more capable and inclined to pursue income decreasing FM in order to produce positive FEs.

Using a sample of 2576 firm- years of companies that are listed on the NYSE on years 2009 and 2010, the study discovers that sell companies conduct income decreasing FM to produce positive FE. However, the frequency of positive FEs of sell companies is not higher than that of buy companies. In addition, in the sell companies group, the companies that have positive forecasts errors issue higher pessimistic forecasts. Such pessimistic forecasts lead to higher positive forecasts errors. However, in the buy companies group, the companies that have positive forecasts errors do not issue higher pessimistic forecasts. Such pessimistic forecasts do not lead to higher positive forecasts errors. Consistent with the efficiency perspective, the study suggests that even though buy and sell companies are highly motivated to avoid negative FEs, they exploit different but efficient strategies in order to meet their respective forecasts.

The findings of this research adds to the previous researches by proving that not only the buy companies (which are supposed to be growth companies) engage in income increasing earnings management to realize positive forecast error, but sell (non-growth) companies engage in negative forecast management to accomplish similar goals. Furthermore, the findings help us understand the complexities behind informative and opportunistic forecasts that fit under efficiency versus opportunistic theories in the literature.

TABLE OF CONTENTS

X

XI

LIST OF SYMBOLS AND ABBREVIATIONS

AR: Analysts' Recommendations

FE: Forecasts Error

FM: Forecasts Management

PSLR: Private Securities Litigation Reform

Reg. FD: Regulation Fair Disclosure

SOX: Sarbanes Oxley Act

EPS: Earnings Per Share

DEFINITIONS OF COMMONLY AND FREQUENTLY USED TERMS

Forecast Management: the action through which the management reports their expectation of EPS at higher or lower levels than their actual expectation.

Forecasts Error: is the difference between the companies' predicted (forecasted) earnings and reported earnings.

Analysts' Recommendations: recommendations of sell analysts that are in one of the five forms of strong buy, buy, hold, sell, and strong sell.

Informative Disclosure: occurs when management report the insider information to the market in a way that will eventually help investors interpret a company's economic prospects, and are believed to reduce the cost of capital.

Efficiency Perspective: is a perspective in financial reporting. In this perspective it is believed that managers, acting as agents, are expected to adopt the most efficiently reflective accounting methods in order to reflect their own performance.

Opportunistic Perspective: holds the opinion that managers, who are agents to the principal, proceed to serve their respective self-interests. They only accept accounting procedures that permit them to benefit, expecting that the firm also gains.

Pessimistic Forecasting: occurs when the management willingly reports lower than real estimate of EPS to the market.

Optimistic Forecasting: occurs when the management willingly reports higher than real estimate of EPS to the market.

Accurate Forecast: is the forecasts that is close to the reported EPS.

Unbiased forecast: is the managers' forecast that would have been reported, if the forecasts management has not taken place. Unbiased forecast is obtained by deducting bias from the reported forecast.

Biased forecast: is the managers' forecast that is reported to the market. This forecast has been manipulated to affect the market expectations.

Reported Forecast: is the forecast that the management reports to the market.

Chapter 1. INTRODUCTION

1.1   Introduction

Financial analysts research macro- and microeconomic conditions together with corporate fundamentals to make business, sector and industry recommendations. They also frequently suggest a course of action, such as to buy or sell a company's shares based on its total present and expected potency. Three main categories of analysts are those that work for ' sell side ' investment companies, those that work for ' buy side ' of investment companies and those who work for investment banks.

Buy side analysts and analysts who work for investment banks evaluate and compare the quality of securities in a given sector or industry for an in-house fund whilst sell side analysts create reports with specific recommendations such as: buy, sell, strong buy, strong sell or hold. These recommendations convey a great deal of weight in the investment industry plus analysts acting inside buy-side firms.

In making their recommendations, analysts will often use financial reports to form expectations regarding a companies' future profit making capabilities. However, since analysts do not usually possess all the pertinent information on a particular company, the company's management is at a distinct advantage when it comes to forming expectations. In other words, analysts could normally only access general public information. To obtain company specific information, the analysts should heavily rely on the information that are disclosed by management. On the other hand, the management has access to both insider and outsider information, their projection of future forecasted profit is arguably more accurate than of analysts and investors in the stock market (2012; Watts & Zimmerman, 1990). When the stock market expectation differs from the management's expectation, they (the managers) will usually adjust that discrepancy using financial disclosures (Abarbanell & Lehavy, 2003a; Dutta & Gigler, 2002).

In accordance with the study conducted by Abarbanell and Lehavy (2003b) this study considers buy stocks as the stocks that are having expected future growth whilst the sell stocks as companies that have low expectation of future growth. It is expected that although both buy companies and sell companies[1] are likely to meet the expectations of the investors, they follow

---

[1] Buy companies are growth type companies and sell companies are non-growth type companies (Abarbanell and Lehavy, 2003).

different strategies to accomplish this aim. This will be explained in the following section.

1.2   Background of the study

Abarbanell and Lehavy (2003b) assume that the companies that analysts recommend to buy (hereafter *buy* companies) are growth type companies that will enjoy high profitability. They show that the management of these companies manage their earnings upwards to meet forecasts and produce positive Forecast Errors (FEs).

In contrast, the incident is not apparent in the companies that analysts recommend to sell (hereafter *sell* companies). According to Abarbanell and Lehavy (2003b), the reasons for such observation are that firstly, sell companies' stock prices are less susceptible to earnings news, making their earnings management ineffective in influencing investors' decisions. In other words, management of sell companies cannot effectively manipulate and increase their profit to boost stock prices. Also secondly, sell companies have insufficient sum of available accounting reserves and pre-managed earnings to achieve any relevant earnings target (Abarbanell &Lehavy, 2003b). This implies that sell companies do not have the sufficient resources to effectively manage earnings.

With regard to the circumstances where managers manage earnings to meet or beat the forecasts, Dutta and Gigler (2002) suggest that both buy and sell companies have strong motivations to avoid negative Forecast Errors (FEs) or/and produce positive FEs. They propose a contractual model in which the managers' utility is mainly based on whether the reported earnings meet or miss the forecasts. Dutta and Gigler's (2002) theoretical model utilizes both forecasts and earnings management to produce positive FEs.

According to Dutta and Gigler (2002), sell companies suffer from communication restriction as their financial resources are limited. Lack of resources will render the sell companies unable to communicate the full scope of their rich information set to investors through the manipulation of reported earnings. Therefore, the communication restrictions bind sell companies. For this reason, sell companies are expected to have different approaches in conveying information to investors compared to buy companies.

On the other hand, issuing high forecasts of earnings help the buy companies in the process of their financial reporting. By having issued high forecasts, they can efficiently manage earnings to meet those forecasts (Dutta and Gigler, 2002; Abarbanell and Lehavy, 2003b). Issuing high forecasts however, does not help the sell companies in the process of their financial reporting, as market punishment could occur as a result of companies missing their forecasts (Burgstahler & Eames, 2006; Dutta & Gigler, 2002;

Matsumoto, 2002). Since the sell companies cannot efficiently manage earnings, they are expected to inevitably issue low forecasts[2].

Such different expectation for the buy and sell companies is consistent with several empirical researches. For example, Barua et al. (2006) confirm that, for the companies that generated profit, compared to the companies that experienced loss, before the earnings management, it is more likely that their pre-managed earnings are less than both analysts' forecasts and prior year period's earning as earnings benchmarks. However, it is more likely for the companies that generated profit to conduct income increasing earnings management and report profits above the benchmarks. Similarly, Kasznik (1999) theorized that it is likely that earnings be managed to an upper forecast than to a lower forecast. Using accruals to gauge earnings management, he found that managers face asymmetric incentives to conduct earnings management. To explain more, Kasznik (1999) found that, managers are more expected to manage their earnings upward rather than downward. This strategy is pursued because the

---

[2] The term forecast management has been broadly used in the literature. There are many papers that used this term. Among these papers are (Bernhardt & Campello, 2007); (Burgstahler & Eames, 2003); (Copeland & Marioni, 1972); (McVay, Nagar, & Tang, 2006).

managers intend to meet forecasts and produce positive earnings surprises.

1.3 Problem Statement

The reason why managers try to beat the forecasts is that by beating the forecasts the market value of the company can be influenced. In explaining such behaviour, prospect theory assumes that decision-makers stem value from gains and losses regarding wealth reference points, rather than from fixed levels of wealth (that is, final outcome)[3] (Kahneman & Tversky, 1979). Such wealth reference points include the managers' earnings forecasts (Burgstahler & Eames, 2006; Matsumoto, 2002). According to Burgstahler and Dichev (1997) the value functions are steepest around the wealth's reference points. In addition, prospect theory advocates that the individuals' value functions are concave in profits and convex in losses with respect to the reference points. This reflects increasing marginal sensitivity to the gains and losses that happens around the reference point. In addition, the value function is also steeper for losses than for gains, which is referred to as loss aversion. This is shown in Figure 1-1.

---

[3] The theory states that people make decisions based on the potential value of losses and gains rather than the final outcome, and that people evaluate these losses and gains using certain heuristics.

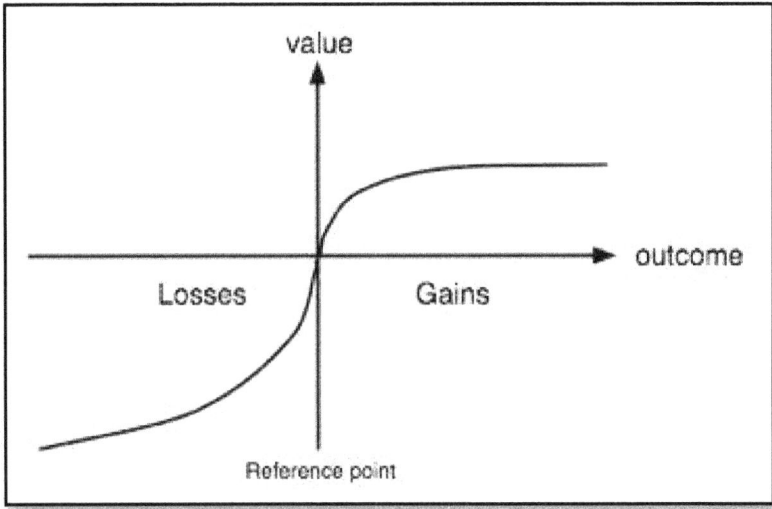

Figure 1-1. Individual value function.
Individual Value function is concave in gains and convex in losses and steepest
around wealth reference point (Burgstahler and Dichev, 1997, Kahneman &
Tversky, 1979).

Assuming the earnings forecasts as reference points (Choi
et al. , 2006; Dutta & Gigler 2002; Burgstahler & Eames, 2006;
Matsumoto, 2002), the Prospect theory can be used to explain why
managers manipulate earnings or forecasts to create positive FEs.
According to the theory, the individual value function is steepest
around the forecasts. Thus, for a given increase in income, the
corresponding increase in value is highest when the increase in
income moves the company from a loss to a gain.

Prospect theory have always been used to explain why managers are always interested to beat the stock market's expectations (Ajinkya & Gift, 1984; Hassell & Jennings, 1986). Since the market value of the company's securities is influenced by the expectation of the net present value of the expected future cash flows (Choi, Myers, Zang, & Ziebart, 2006, p. 239), beating expectations will most definitely increase share price.

Due to the fact that the management's compensation is either in the form of cash bonus on any increases in share price, options or shares in the firm (Choi et al., 2006, p. 224), the increase in share price will greatly benefit the management. This is in line with the "Positive Accounting Theory" of Watts and Zimmerman (1990) which assumes that in an agency setting, all actions by all individuals, including managers (agents), are primarily driven by self-interest.

Consistent with self interest in Positive Accounting Theory (Graham, Harvey, & Rajgopal, 2005), the Agency Theory (Deegan & Unerman, 2006) also shares the view that in the management's share based compensation or option-based compensation, if the management's interests are aligned with the increase in stock prices, then the management (agent) will be motivated to raise the investors (principle) interests (Choi et al., 2006, p. 224). However, this approach is criticized because it may tempt managers to pass *inaccurate information* to stockholders and other stock market participants, with the intention of increasing stock prices (Watts & Zimmerman, 1990). In this regard, Deegan and Unerman (2006) and Choiet al. (2006, p. 226) state that the Positive Accounting Theory assumes that since all actions by all individuals are driven by self-interest, if management is rewarded on the basis of accounting numbers, then they will have an incentive to manipulate such numbers to their own end.

As a response to the concerns on the conflict of interest between the management and investors, there have been some efforts in codification strict rules to place the management's benefit to be in line with the investors' interests among these efforts is the enactment of Sarbanes Oxley[4], 2002 (Jensen & Meckling, 1976). As Arping and Sautner (2007) state, Sarbanes Oxley is one of the most significant corporate disclosure and governance improvements in US history. The primary objective of Sarbanes Oxley, (2002) (SOX) is "to protect investors by improving the accuracy and reliability of corporate disclosures".

However, numerous studies showed that generally, the management will not fully reveal accurate information to the

---

[4]Sarbanes–Oxley act was enacted in United States on 2002; it improved standards for all U.S. public company boards, management and public accounting firms. It includes topics such as auditor independence, corporate governance, internal control assessment, and enhanced financial disclosure.

market. For example, Xin (2005) confirmed that management manipulate the reported earnings to meet the analysts' forecasts, and Barua et al. (2010) also showed that the management engage in earnings management to meet benchmarks. Burgstahler and Eames (2007) proposed that managers sacrifice long-term growth and permanent value increasing opportunities to avoid short term negative FEs.[5]

This view of forgoing long-term growth and permanent value increasing opportunities to avoid short term negative FEs fits the Watts and Zimmerman (2006) *opportunistic perspective* and is consistent with criticisms on aligning the managers' interest with an increase in stock prices that is advocated by Jensen and Meckling (2007). The theories of forecasts management[6] associated with this view have primarily modelled the forecasts as an opportunity that the managers will use to pre-empt litigation

---

[5]FEs can have a vast influence on a company's stock price. Several studies propose that positive FEs not only produces an immediate hike in a stock's price, but also to a gradual increase over time (Kinney, Burgstahler, & Martin, 2002; Skinner & Sloan, 2002). Hence, it is not surprising that some managers are known for regularly beating earning forecasts. This can even happen at the expense of having less long-term growth such as cutting R&D costs in order to increase the earnings and meet the forecasts.

[6] The word forecast management is a well-established term in the literature. Several seminal papers like (Bernhardt & Campello, 2007), (Burgstahler & Eames, 2003), (Copeland & Marioni, 1972), (McVay et al., 2006) use the term forecasts management. Forecast management is the action through which the management reports their expectation of EPS at higher or lower levels than their actual expectation.

concerns, influence their reputation and produce positive FEs while simultaneously affecting stock prices (Burgstahler & Eames, 2006).

For example, Baik and Jiang (1978) state that the company uses the earnings estimates to dampen the market expectations. They find that managers successfully reduce the expectations to an achievable level. In fact, by pre-empting bad news that results from negative FEs management reduces the expected cost of litigation.

Similarly, Das et al. (2012) state that since stock prices are susceptible to managers' forecasts, the management is likely to report a higher forecast. On the other hand, stock price is highly susceptible to the managers' FEs (Baik & Jiang, 2006; Das, Kyonghee, & Sukesh, 2008). Thus, the more negative the FE is (reported earnings is less than predicted earnings), the more it is conceived as a sign of bad news, and such bad news will most definitely lead to a dramatic fall of stock price (Bartov, Givoly, & Hayn, 2002; Kasznik & McNichols, 2002). In order to prevent such incident, the management is inclined to engage in practices like deliberately decreasing the forecasts, which is called producing downward biased forecast, whilst increasing the reported profit, in order to beat forecasts and create positive FEs (Brown & Caylor, 2005; Gong, Li, & Xie, 2009; Kasznik, 1999a).

In summary, the opportunistic view of Forecast Management (FM) is said to take place when the forecasted earning vary from the actual management expectation; that is, when an agent fraudulently communicate private information. Such opportunistic view, however, fails to correspond to the revelation principle (Burgstahler & Dichev, 1997; Demski, 1998; Dye, 1988; Evans & Sridhar, 1996) and expectation adjustment hypothesis (Graham et al., 2005). This will be explained in the subsequent paragraphs.

The Revelation principle states that any feasible equilibrium results of any feasible mechanism, however complicated, can be reproduced by a truth-telling equilibrium results of a mechanism under which the agents are required to state their private information (Dye, 1988). In other words, when the revelation principle is valid, any balance that comprises non-truthful reporting (i.e., ones where forecasts management is happening) can always be ruled by one where truth telling is brought (Evans & Sridhar, 1996).

Based on this principle, in the agent-principle model of the firm, in order for a rational communication strategy to be stimulated for an agent, the managers, acting as an agent, should reveal the correct private information to the market. Dye (1988, page 200) observes that "when the manager can communicate all dimensions of his private information to the shareholders, the Revelation Principle does indeed apply, and so no internal demand exists for manipulative reporting."

According to the expectation adjustment hypothesis (Deegan & Unerman, 2006; Graham et al., 2005, p. 231), when the stock market expectation differs from the management's expectation, they (the management) will usually adjust that discrepancy using financial disclosures. This corresponds with the efficiency perspective which states that managers, acting as agents, are predicted to adopt the most efficiently reflective accounting methods to reflect their own performance (Farrell, 2005).

Deegan and Unerman (2005) state that a great deal of positive accounting researches adopted the efficiency perspective. This perspective proposes that managers will choose to use a particular accounting method because it will most efficiently provide a record of how the organization actually performs. The managers will use forecasts to pass insider information to outsiders. In fact, by forecasting earnings, information asymmetry is reduced, leading to a reduction in the company's cost of capital (Lev and Penman, 1990). In this regard, Jensen and Meckling (2007) argue that the practice of providing true financial statements actually leads to real cost savings, as it enables organizations to attract funds at an overall lower cost. As a result of true and reliable financial reporting, external parties will have more reliable information about the resources and obligations of the organization, enabling the organization to attract funds at a lower cost that would otherwise be possible, which will increase the overall value of the organization (Xin, 2007). When the company's financial position is satisfactory, their inclination to convey a more positive information to shareholders will increase, and this will increase the management's prediction's frequency (Arya, Glover, & Sunder, 1998). Hence, issuing earnings' prediction restricts the management's ability to conduct earnings management, i.e. they cannot manage earnings in a desirable direction. In fact, earnings forecasts actually lead to less earnings management (Cotter, Tuna, & Wysocki, 2010). This view is under efficiency perspective which will be broadly explained in chapter 2.

The opportunistic and efficiency views of the forecasts undertaken by the managers are completely different. In the efficiency view, it is assumed that by providing accurate forecasts, the management provides accurate information to the market, hence, restricting them to conduct earnings management. Thus, the forecasts are true. In contrast, the opportunistic view of forecasts is that the management's forecasts is made of biased signs. The managers will use earnings and forecasts management as means to make positive earnings surprise that will produce a short-term stock price increase, or inhibit its decrease.

By using a framework that revelation principle holds, this research shows that as indicated by the companies' growth capabilities, the analysts' recommendations explain the difference in the behaviours of managers within both views. The research hypothesise that the management's decide to conduct FM to generate positive FE in certain circumstances but eschew FM when those circumstances are absent. More specifically, this research determines how the analysts' recommendations of strong buy and strong sell can explain the manager's forecast management behaviour.

When the company's financial situation is satisfactory and the company has growth capability (buy companies), management's inclination to convey positive (true) information to shareholders will increase, and this will increase the management's prediction's optimism ; (Hui, Matsunaga, & Morse, 2009; Jensen & Meckling, 1976).

Consistent with Dutta and Gigler's (2002) model, for buy companies, the forecasts convey the management's true expectation to the market that is followed by income increasing earnings management. However, for the sell companies, the forecasts do not convey true (or optimistic) information to the market, but, it is used to dampen the market expectation so that the management can benefit from a positive stock price shock, which is the result of positive FE.

This research highlights the factor relating to the companies' growth status that influence the management's decision to report pessimistic forecast to produce positive FE when company's shares are recommended to sell, and generate optimistic forecast when company's shares are recommended to buy. More specifically, this research determines the ability of analysts' recommendations (in terms of buy or sell recommendations) in explaining the reason behind FM.

The importance of the problem is that while studies that consider opportunistic view of forecasts do not comply with the revelation principle, this thesis is going to address this problem using the model developed by Dutta and Gigler (2002) as a basis, in which the revelation principle is adhered to.

In the agent-principal model, the revelation principle is of immense significance in the search for answers. The researcher have to only explore the group of equilibria characterized by inducement compatibility. That is, if the researcher needs to apply certain results or property, he might bound his exploration to procedures in which agents are set to disclose their private information to the principal that ensures that effect or property. If no such open and straight system occurs, no system can affect this result/property.

In the agent-principal model, the principal intend to state their activities on the basis of information privately comprehended to the agent (management). For example, the principal want to know the right expectation about company's future performances. He is not able to study everything merely by referring to the agent released information, since it is in the agent interest to misrepresent the truth. Fortunately, when the revelation principle is hold, the principal may create a game whose rules can impact agent to play the way that the information is not distorted.

In the absence of revelation principle, the principal's dilemma would be hard to resolve. He would be required to to study all the feasible games and select the one that best effects other players' tactics. Moreover, the principal would have to draw conclusions from the management reports that can show false information to him. According to the revelation principle, the principal should only care about games where agents honestly report their private information.

In Dutta and Gigler's (2002) model, the managers' forecast is considered as a form of voluntary disclosure. Forecasts management is said to occur when the management issues forecasts that deviate from their actual expectation. This research considers the agent's private information regarding economic earnings and his capability to express them via earnings forecasts. Like the agency models of Christensen (2001) and Dye (2009), the true revelation of the self-reported information (earnings estimates) is implemented through reported accounting earnings. In this context, the reported accounting earnings thus serve a confirmatory role in disciplining the manager's earnings estimates. This modelling method has a apparent advantage: it does not need a infringement of the Revelation Principle[7] in order to make a need for forecasts management, and this is what most of opportunistic forecast management literatures failed to achieve.

1.4   Research Questions

Following the model developed by Dutta and Gigler (2002), in which forecast is considered as a tool for conveying true information and using the agency setting to characterise the association between the company's shareholders and the manager, the association between the companies' growth capability and forecasts management will be tested. Following the study in Abarbanell and Lehavy (2003b) the companies' growth capability is represented by analysts' recommendations. The analysts' recommendations come in the form of buy and sell recommendations to the investors in the stock market. That is, the analysts may recommend the investors to either buy or sell the stocks of the companies. It is assumed that the companies that the analysts recommend their stocks as buy (buy recommendations or buy companies) are the companies that have high growth

---

[7]As mentioned earlier, the revelation principle is important in finding solutions to the agent-principal model. By using this principal, if the researcher desires to apply some effect or property, he can limit his quest to mechanisms in which agents are eager to disclose their private information to the principal that has that effect or property. If no such direct and straightforward mechanism exists, no mechanism can apply this outcome/property.

capabilities and the companies that analysts recommend to sell (sell companies) are the companies that does not have high growth capabilities.

Thus, the research questions of this study consist of the following questions:

(1) Do the managers in sell companies manage the forecasted earnings downwards to a greater extent than buy companies?

(2) Do the managers in sell companies have higher positive FEs than buy companies?

(3) Do the managers in sell companies manage the forecasted earnings downward to achieve positive FEs?

(4) Does the management of buy companies conduct income decreasing FM to achieve positive FEs?

1.5 Objective

The major objective of this research is to examine the effects of analysts' recommendations (which represent the growth and non-growth companies) on the managers' decisions towards FM. By understanding the factors influencing the managers' behaviour towards FM, this research contributes in explaining the different views regarding the optimistic and pessimistic forecasts in previous studies. Accordingly, this research is set to determine whether the analysts' recommendations can explain the reason behind the differences in the strategies that the managers choose in relation to forecasted earnings. More specifically, the aims of this research are as follows:

(a) To examine whether management of *sell companies* tend to actively engage in managing the forecasted earnings downward compared to management of *buy companies.*

(b) To examine whether management of *sell companies* are more likely to achieve positive FEs than management of *buy companies.*

(c) To examine the effect of the analysts' recommendation on the managers' decisions of producing downward biased forecasts to reach positive FEs.

1.6   Significance of the Research

In a literature review of FM, Hirst et al. (2008) concluded that predict characteristics appeared to be the least well-understood element of earnings estimates-both in terms of theory and empirical research - even if it is the element over which management has the highest control.

Getting an improved grasp of the selections that the management make once they decide to issue an earnings forecast is an important direction for both theory development and empirical research (Beyer, Cohen, Lys, & Walther, 2010; Hirst et al., 2008). Therefore, chances exist for theory improvement on the selections that the managers make in relation to forecast qualities. As a result of less theories, it is no wonder that compared with the huge works on forecast predecessors and outcomes, relatively less studies assess how managers select the features of their earnings estimates. The absence of theory could explain why the studies that has been directed on forecast charactristics are relatively recent (at least relative to research on forecast antecedents and consequences) (Beyer et al., 2010; Hirst et al., 2008). Therefore, the reason this research is conducted is that while existing theories emphasizes informative characteristic of the forecasts, these theories have been followed by a mixed empirical findings about the nature of the forecasts. By considering the analysts' recommendations as the factors that explains the managers' behaviour towards forecasted earnings, this research extends the understanding on the nature of forecasts and the role played by the analysts' recommendations in influencing this behaviour.

1.7   Scope of the study

In the weak efficient markets, insider accounting information might affect the stock price before it is publicly released to the market. Therefore reported information does not significantly reflect the stock prices. However, in the efficient market, release of new accounting information affects the market expectation about the future performances (Epstein & Schneider,

2008). This creates an opportunity for the managers to manipulate the accounting information in an attempt to influence market expectations. Since the efficiency of U.S. market has been frequently confirmed by several researches (Fama, 1998; Hirst et al., 2008; Li & Ding, 2008), this study focuses on the U.S. stock market. The semi-strong efficiency of the U.S. stock market provides a desirable sample to examine the management desire to manipulate the outsiders' expectation, thus, the market chosen for sampling is New York Stock Exchange (NYSE).

1.8 Summary

This chapter explained the incidence of FM, as well as the views on forecasts management namely the efficiency and opportunistic perspectives. Following that, the chapter explains analysts' recommendations as a factor that could explain the mixed findings thus far. I explained the research objective as determining whether the analysts' recommendations can explain the reason behind the differences in the strategies that the managers choose in relation to forecasted earnings. Based on this research objective, I explained the research questions. Finally I explained that the scope of the study is the US market.

1.9 Chapter organization

The remainder of the thesis is organized as follows. The next chapter, Chapter 2 discusses the history of forecasts management in U.S. along with the theories and empirical researches. Chapter 3 explains the theoretical framework, hypotheses, and research methods used in the study. Chapter 4 presents and discusses the empirical results. Chapter 5 concludes the overall results, acknowledges limitations inherent in the scope of study and research design and identifies additional potential issues for future research.

Chapter 2. LITERATURE REVIEW

2.1 Introduction

This chapter discusses some of the previous empirical findings on opportunistic and informative views of forecasts. The theories to support the opportunistic and informative views on managers' forecasts are presented to explain why the companies that have different analysts' recommendations are expected to behave differently toward issuing optimistic or pessimistic forecasts.

Namely, revelation principle and the expectation adjustment hypothesis will be used to support informative forecasts, while also using the prospect theory and transaction cost theory to explain the management decision to meet forecasts and produce positive earnings surprises that have been documented in the literature. Furthermore, Dutta and Gigler's (2002) theoretical framework will be used to explain the behaviour of buy and sell companies.

After explaining the theories, the chapter further highlights the main factors that affect the reliability of managers' forecasts. Finally, this chapter concludes by highlighting some of the findings in the literature that support the presumed relationship of stock price and forecasts management.

24

2.2　Voluntary Disclosure

The SEC compels publicly traded companies to reveal specific information to the society. Instances of such compulsory disclosure are annual reports and earnings announcements. Besides compulsory disclosures, companies voluntarily reveal material news to the society. An example of a voluntary disclosure is managers' estimates of earnings. Previous literature documents several incentives for voluntary disclosure.

Ajinkya and Gift (1984) examine if managers voluntarily predicted earnings to amend the market's anticipation of the company's future earnings. They present that managers willingly disclose private information, both good news and bad news, to the public to reduce the information asymmetry between management and investors. They further demonstrate that market responds to managers ' estimates and amend its anticipation of company's future earnings consequently.

Trueman (1986) creates a model presenting that managers willingly issue forecasted earnings to indicate their ability to forecast future revenue. Trueman claims that the market assesses a company based on its manager's ability to predict future economic changes and the ability to amend the company's production plans for the future variations. This gives managers with inducements to reveal both good news and bad news immediately to increase the company's value, if there is no harm for creating an earnings forecast.

Nagar et al. (2003) investigate whether stock price-based compensation produces motivations for managers to immediately reveal private information to the market. They claim and realize that managers with higher levels of stock price-based compensation are more possible to issue earnings projections, since stock mispricing could have a undesirable effect on their wealth. In addition, they realize that executives disclose both good news and bad news for the market immediately, since the market responds to good news predictions positively and interprets silence as bad news.

2.3   Managers' Earnings Forecasts

An extensive managers' forecast literature has examined various issues relevant to managers' forecasts. These studies have tested the elements of managers' forecast accuracy, precision, venue, and timing, and consequences of managers' forecasts for analysts, investors, and security prices.

Baginski et al. (1993) show a relationship between the accuracy of managers' earnings forecasts and their level of certainty. Managers who have a higher degree of certainty about earnings issue more accurate earnings forecasts. Likewise those incidents and environmental issues that contribute to uncertainty result in less accuracy and precision in managers' earnings forecasts (Baginski, Hassell, & Wieland, 2011).

Previous researches have focused on the association of managers' prediction to financial analysts forecasts adjustments (Baginski & Hassell, 1990; Brushko, 2013), equity valuation (Baginski, 1987; Demers & Vega, 2013; Emami, Amini, & Emami, 2012; Knauer & Wömpener, 2011), auditor quality (Dhaliwal, Lamoreaux, Lennox, & Mauler, 2014; Knauer & Wömpener, 2011; Stein, 1998), earnings management (Kasznik, 1999b), and the influence on other companies in the industry (Baginski, 1987).

Studies have examined the effect of prior managers' forecast accuracy on investor expectations (Baginski, 1987; Hirst, Koonce, & Miller, 1999) and managers' forecast as warnings in the face of earnings surprise (Kasznik & Lev, 1995). Hirst et al. (1999) provide evidence that investor expectations are influenced by prior managers' forecast accuracy.

Most earnings projection studies fit into a three-stage model of voluntary disclosure developed by King et al. (1990). The first decision that managers need to make is whether to voluntarily reveal earnings projections or other information. The second choice in their model is whether to grant private forecast through analysts or used public channels.

27

Communicating information with only analysts is precluded by Regulation Fair Disclosure thus this option and decision point is no longer a concern. The last decision in their model, "tertiary choices regarding public forecast disclosure," is concerned with the details of the disclosure such as precision, venue, timing, and ancillary information.

Early papers (Patell 1976, Ainkya and Gift 1984) showed that managers' earnings forecasts move markets, i.e., are new information to the markets. Like other disclosures, both voluntary and compulsory, managers' earnings forecasts decrease information asymmetry and, consecutively, reduce investor uncertainty and ultimately lower the costs of capital to the company.

The impact of management earnings forecasts to lower the costs of capital is of particular importance to companies (Hurwitz, 2012). Companies that have the greatest information asymmetry can benefit the most by reducing that asymmetry. On the other hand, the accumulation of the information required to make predictions is expensive. Arguably, the non-growth companies may be motivated to issue conservative and less optimistic earnings forecasts. This is because of the deficiency of the resources they have to manipulate the earnings in order to meet the forecasts.

2.4 Necessity of Managers' Forecasts in Relation to Market Expectations

It has been argued that the disclosure of managers' forecasts of future profits or cash flows would be very advantageous to investors along with managers. The advantages are explained as follows:

2.4.1.1 *Importance of managers' forecasts for security pricing*

Since investment decisions by management are made in the context of the expectations which they hold of the profitability of future operations, the disclosure of their forecasts would represent the essential information needed by investors.

The release of company forecasts would supply investors with the advantage of management's knowledge of company operations, and its opinions of the future outlook for such operations. Market efficiency does not imply clairvoyance. Therefore, since much information concerning a company's future prospects and plans is not made public, it may be assumed not to be impounded already in share prices. Therefore, it may be argued that the publication of company forecasts would result in more efficient share prices (Cohen, Marcus, Rezaee, & Tehranian, 2011). Such stock prices will reveal more accurately the future outlooks of the company, and the worth of the company's shares. Patell (2006) examined the reaction of share prices to the voluntary disclosure of forecasts of annual earnings per share by 336 companies, and found that, on average, there was a significant share price reaction in the week when forecasts were disclosed. In fact, share price will adjust to the information content of the managers' forecasts. Therefore, it can be said that, the public disclosure of information (like forecasts) which are relevant to investors' needs might help prevent abnormal returns accruing to privileged individuals having access to inside information.

2.4.1.2 *Managers' forecasts as performance benchmark*

A large body of accounting literature has established that analysts' forecasts are important earnings benchmarks. Studies show that the market rewards firms for meeting or beating analysts' earnings expectations (Bartov et al., 2002; Lopez & Rees, 2002). Another stream of accounting literature documents that voluntary managers' forecasts, despite credibility concerns, cause analysts and the market to revise their expectations. In particular, evidence suggests that managers often use their disclosures intentionally to guide analysts' expectations down (Cotter, Tuna and Wysocki, 2006; Baik and Jiang, 2006; and Li, 2008) if they believe these expectations are unattainable (Versano & Trueman, 2013).

Libby and Tan (1999) study analysts' reaction to short-horizon managers' guidance with respect to bad news only and find that when managers provide guidance, analysts' expectations of future earnings are higher than they would be without the guidance, thus implying that guidance has a positive impact on analysts' forecasts.

In a related study, Dhole, Mishra et al. (2010) evaluate the relative importance of managers' forecasts and analysts' forecasts as performance benchmarks especially when analysts and managers appear to disagree. They find that when managers' forecasts and the subsequent analyst forecasts are different, although the market might view both the benchmarks as being important, the market's expectations are shaped more significantly by managers' forecasts than by analysts' forecasts. Finally they conclude that, the market treat managers' forecasts as important performance benchmarks (Dhole et al., 2010).

Similarly, Caylor, Lopez and Rees (2007) find, in the context of analysts' forecasts, that reporting a positive earnings surprise at the earnings announcement date is not necessarily the best disclosure strategy. Their results support Kahneman and Tversky's (1979) prospect theory. Moreover, Dhole, Mishra et al. (2010) state that managers may act to meet or beat their own expectations, rather than the more recent analysts' forecasts (Dhole et al., 2010).

Similarly Pinello (2004) conjectures and finds evidence that analysts' forecasts do not truly capture investors' expectations, thus leading some credence to the claim that analysts' forecasts are not the only performance benchmark. Similarly Das et al. (2010) find that the consensus analyst forecast routinely disagrees with managers' forecasts. They find that this disagreement causes investors to discount the earnings surprise by as much as 37%.

Thus, it is believed that the disclosure of corporate plans and managers' forecasts would provide investors with a better basis for assessing managerial performance. The market appears to treat managers' forecasts as important performance benchmarks. In addition, the market's expectations appear to be shaped significantly by managers' forecasts (Dhole et al., 2010).

2.5 Managers' Forecasts Beneficial to the Firm

2.5.1 Returns Based Benefits of Managers' Earnings Forecasts

The previous discussion has indicated that managers' earnings forecasts may lead to price changes in line with the news enclosed in the forecasts. While this suggests that managers may use forecasts as a means to reveal their opinions, Ajinkya and Gift (1984) formalize this by suggesting an "expectations adjustment hypothesis" that claims managers use forecasts to change market expectations in the direction of their own beliefs in the events where expectations vary greatly. They examine the theory with analyst expectations, managers' earnings forecasts and market returns. Their results verify the expectation adjustment hypothesis, offering proof for the idea that a major advantage of forecasting is to bring the market expectations in line with managerial expectations.

Das, Kim and Patro (2008) further examine the capability of managers' earnings forecasts to line up market and management expectations by considering returns shapes in periods following the forecasts. They provide evidence of a drift succeeding managers' earnings forecasts that proposes the market does not properly accredit the information on the time of the forecasts. Nevertheless, they obtain firm support that the managers' earnings forecasts were useful at decreasing the market reaction to the earnings "surprise" that happens at the time of the earnings announcement.

Along with the Skinner and Sloan's (2002) proof of great negative market responses near earnings surprises, the current research shows managers' earnings forecasts can benefit managers to keep away from market consequences.

Likewise, Coller and Yohn (1997) emphasize on the period after release of managers' earnings forecasts, but their research explores information asymmetry by means of bid-ask spreads. They realize that spreads grow up for to two days after the forecasts, but then fall and stay lower until the related earnings announcement. Therefore, along with altering mean expectations, managers' earnings forecasts seem to decrease asymmetry among market participants.

A number of further researches also look at how managers' earnings forecasts may alter the patterns of upcoming returns or other returns related elements. These researches try to develop the earlier discussed literatures by investigating formerly recognized returns events and then indicating ways wherein forecasts may influence the information environment and consequently the outline of returns. Choi, Myers, Zang and Ziebart (2008) indicate that the present period market returns are more reflective of upcoming performance for companies that report forecasts. They find this relation is greater for companies that report short-term/quarterly forecasts even after conditioning on reporting broader range of forecasts. Thus, not only can managers' earnings forecasts "pull understanding forward" but it can be seen that reporting a longer term forecasts over different prospects seems to produce a greater insight for the market.

Li and Tse (2008) choose a different method by investigating whether managers' forecasts can influence the returns pattern produced by the "post-earnings announcement drift". They find that announcing managers' forecasts concurrent with reporting earnings considerably decreases the drift – especially if the company has a history of previous accurate forecasts. Managers' forecasts reported alone are less actual and in fact, produce an earnings flow themselves. Li and Tse (2008) presume that the way managers' forecasts are reported with other information or reported separately makes a significant difference in their effect on returns flow.

Finally, Pownall and Waymire (1989) indicate the companies that report forecasts experience a smaller amount of information transmit from information events of other companies in their industry. This shows that reporting managers' forecasts lets managers to guide the market more distinctly on the information belonging to their company, rather than to have the company considered as a harmonized part of the industry.

In sum, these returns based papers indicate that managers' forecasts can have an extensive effect on how investors see the firm. These effects are consistent with managers' forecasts facilitating the market to recognize the broader range effects of present firm performance and at decreasing asymmetry among investors. Clearly, these abilities imply the managers' forecasts are able to give important aids for managers trying to grow an updated set of investors.

In spite of this sound proof, it is worthy to indicate that not all returns based researches realize a positive effect for managers' forecasts. For instance, Rogers et al. (2009) investigate the effect on options volatility. They show that overall there is trivial or no effect. However, for managers' forecasts that include negative news volatility may grow— in line with the managers' forecasts leading to market ambiguity. This is in line with Bushee and Noe

(2000) who investigate the effect of disclosure on the whole (not only managers' forecasts) and show that heightened quantities are related to greater consequent volatility and with catching the attention of investors who frequently churn the stock analyst associated benefits of providing managers' earnings forecasts.

Whereas majority of papers have aimed on investigating managers' forecasts effect on share prices, there is also a literature that investigates the association between managers' forecasts and analyst forecast errors. Because of the significant role of analysts in steering market expectations and as an audience for disclosure on the whole, it is helpful to extend an insight of how managers' forecasts affect managers' interactions with analysts.

Cotter, Tuna and Wysocki (2006) indicate that it is more probable that managers provide forecasts when analyst are optimistic and when the analyst forecast diffusion is low. That is, managers' forecasts are used to discontinue a strong analyst consensus of higher performance than management expects. They show that analyst react by rapidly adjusting their earnings expectations downward. Like a number of the returns based researches; this is another example that indicates how managers' forecasts can be applied to help managers in adjusting poorly informed market views. However, it indicates that managers' forecasts can offer an supplementary lever through also influencing analysts insights.

In related research, Hutton (2005) compares companies that provide forecasts to those that do not. She shows that there are a number of motives managers give such forecasts, such as an earnings process that is fundamentally complicated or a great level of analyst following. All of the motives are in line with managers believing the necessity to capture the company's expectations when there is a set of concerned parties and the information is hard to forecast, in line with a management effort to effectively manage the company's information environment.

Analyst forecasts are more precise for companies that guide, proposing that generally the practice leads to improved information in the market. In addition, the anticipations are more pessimistic, showing managers might be intentionally biasing the forecast to raise the probability that they will meet or beat forecasts. Whilst such partiality is less than suitable from the essence of a completely informed market, it is probably a logical managerial reaction to the significant penalization to missing earnings expectations (Cheong & Thomas, 2013; Skinner & Sloan, 2002). Once more, this proof indicates managers efficiently utilizing forecasts to take the reins of the company's information setting.

2.5.2 Litigation Linked Advantages of Disclosure

Managers' earnings forecasts are frequently regarded as a possible reason for lawsuit and experts often maintain that their advisors recommend not in favour of reporting any forecasts. Along with these circumstantial claims, the previous researches have established that managers' earnings forecasts are more probable in areas with lower legal risk (Johnson, Kasznik and Nelson, 2001; Baginski, Hassell and Kimbrough, 2002).

In spite of the proof of litigation risk preventing managers' earnings forecasts, researches particularly investigating the role of litigation and managers' forecasts indicate the managers' forecasts may be a useful tool in handling lawsuit threat. Managers are expected to issue short term forecast to deter bad earnings news (Skinner, 1994; Soffer, Thiagarajan, and Walther, 2000). Although there is diverse evidence about whether the forecasts decrease the possibility of being called in a litigation (Francis, Philbrick and Schipper, 1994; Field, Lowry and Shu, 2005) they do decrease the extent and possibility of a pay-out when there is lawsuit (Skinner, 1997). Collectively, these studies propose managers' forecasts show a significant role in lawsuit. In addition, they are additional support of managers by means of management FEs control the firm's reporting setting and of its associated financial outcomes.

In addition, the study conducted by Cornerstone Research proposes that lawsuits are caused by significant share price declines (Cornerstone, 2008). The discussion of management FE studies in earlier sections of this chapter has indicated it can produce more up-to-date and well-ordered market expectations of performance. This proposes that management FEs can prevent lawsuit by decreasing the likelihood of a significant stock price drop.

2.6   Credibility of Managers' Earnings Forecasts

Credibility is a main issue in defining the market influence of managers' earnings forecasts. Jennings (1987) indicated the market and analysts reactions to managers' earnings forecasts are greatly linked. Namely, once analysts amend their own forecasts to be harmonious with managers' earnings forecasts, the market is more expected to react as if the managers' earnings forecasts are credible. This proposes some reliable, efficient procedure for verifying the basic reliability of managers' earnings forecasts.

Prior researches have demonstrated that managers who provide more accurate information are rated as more credible (Tan et al. 2002). Hirst et al. (1999) found that forecast form affected investors' confidence in earnings forecasts, especially when managers were viewed as accurate in their prior forecasts. Moreover, prior research has shown that market and analyst reactions are stronger for firms that provide more accurate forecasts (Baginski et al. 1993; Pownall et al. 1993; Bamber & Cheon 1998; Hutton & Stocken 2007; Ng, Tuna & Verdi 2008).

2.6.1 Investor Reliance on Managers' Forecasts

There have been several studies which provide evidence concerning the relation between disclosure forthcomingness and management's reporting reliability in the short-term (Libby and Tan 1999; Tan et al. 2002, Mercer 2005). All of these studies have found evidence which suggests that managers who provide more forthcoming disclosures are rated as more credible than managers who are less forthcoming. For example, Libby and Tan (1999) find that investors' assessments of manager's integrity are higher when managers provide warnings about unexpected earnings. Similarly, Tan et al. (2002) found that in the short-term, managers who provide more accurate disclosures are regarded by analysts as more forthcoming, having greater integrity, and are regarded as more competent. Mercer (2005) found that in the short-term, managers who provided more forthcoming disclosure were rated by investors as more credible than those who did not.

The next section describes manipulating the forecasts to affect the stock prices.

2.6.2 Managing Forecasts to Affect Stock Prices

Apart from manipulating forecasts to alleviate the litigation pressure from investors (section 3-5-2), another reason why managers engage more in forecast management is to manipulate stock prices. Kasznik and McNichols (1998) and Bartov et al.

(1988) found that meeting expectations is beneficial for a firm's stock price, even after restraining the effect of earnings news in the season, and the day of reported earnings. One of the findings of their research is that the earnings management that is done in the performance year, which is along the season or the year, has slighter effect on profit than the earnings news, which is revealed at the time of reporting earnings (Downing and Sharpe 2003).

Furthermore, Das, Kyonghee, & Sukesh (1997) suggested that earnings management and expectation management, whether used together or interchangeably, will produce increase in stock prices. Beyer (2000) also showed that there is a great relation between forecasts, earnings and stock prices. He further showed that the balancing price for the company is a function of the management's forecast, reported earnings and the square of management earnings forecast error. Moreover, he shows that a firm's stock price is more sensitive to a firm's real earnings than to its management's forecast. Finally, he showed that after controlling for reported earnings and the degree of earnings surprises, at an earning reporting date, if the company has positive earnings surprise, the stock price will be higher than compared to the case in which the company has negative earnings surprises (Payne & Robb, 2000).

In accordance with this view of earnings forecast leading to a decrease in the company's cost of capital, Frankel and

McNichols and Wilson showed that when the company accesses the capital market, managers are more tempted to forecast earnings. Furthermore, Coller and Yohn (2002) discovered that stock ask and bids spread will decrease significantly in 21 days around the management earnings forecast date (Pinello, 2004).

Ahmed et al. (2005) documented that market participants, to some extent, are aware of managers' intention to reverse unsatisfactory news in favour of optimistic news, which agrees with the facts stipulated above. They found no evidence that investors systematically overvalue extreme accruals, and no evidence that the companies that avoid losses or income decrease has more extreme accruals than the others. Also Cormier & Martinez (1997) documented that in the year in which the company's reported earning is manipulated, French investors did not readjust the market value of the firm and reported earnings. This can weaken the market incentives that are behind earnings management.

2.6.3   Information Surprise

The surprise of the information contained in the forecast is the difference between the investor's current level of belief based on the information set currently held and the new information in the forecast. Surprise is a measure of the amount of information asymmetry among management and investors.

Surprise also represents the maximum belief revision management expects to generate with its disclosure, since the purpose of its disclosure is to bring investors' expectations in line with its own. Management's expectation that it can change beliefs is supported by studies in psychology that have found that a portion of a subject's opinion change is a function of the difference between the current beliefs a subject has and the beliefs advocated by a communicator (Hovland & Pritzker, 1957). Greater opinion changes occur when the difference between the subject's beliefs and the communicator's advocated message is larger. Surprise has also been referred to as the degree of conformity.

The next section explains the information surprise that occurs when the management beats the previously reported forecast.

2.6.4   Importance of Positive earnings Surprises

Reasons for empirically observed valuation consequences of positive earnings surprises have been pondered but left unsolved. Bartov et al. (2002) pose two likely reasons for the premium to meeting or beating forecasts. First, investors may be react excessively to occurrences of meeting or beating the forecast. In this case, Bartov et al. argue that a market adjustment should be perceived in following periods. However, they find no proof of a turnaround of the premium in following periods and thus reject investor overreaction as a possible justification.

Bartov et al. (2002) instead argue for the alternative explanation that the firm's achievement in meeting or beating the forecast is informative in regard to upcoming firm performance. To support their argument, Bartov et al. document positive associations between meeting or beating the forecast and metrics of future firm performance (including return-on-assets, return-on-equity, and occurrence of losses, market-to-book-ratio, profit margin, and earnings growth). Bartov et al. claim that investors are sensible in the allocation of a premium to firms that meet or beat forecasts because the firm's present achievement is revealing with regard to upcoming performance. In making this implication, however, the writers suppose that investors are conscious of this practical consistency.

Similarly, by considering annual numbers, Kasznik and McNichols (2002) claim that if firms that meet or beat the latest prediction have greater incomes in upcoming years and investors predict this, a reward to meeting or beating the forecast may solely be attributable to greater anticipated upcoming earnings. While Kasznik and McNichols (2002) verify that firms that meet or beat expectations have considerably greater earnings forecasts and recognized earnings than firms that do not succeed to meet expectations, their results also imply that the market reward is incremental to the greater upcoming incomes that could reasonably be anticipated by shareholders based on past incomes. Caylor et al. (2003) present additional proof that the premium to meeting or beating the forecast can be only partially explained as a sign of upcoming performance.

Bernhardt and Campello (2002) also speculate as to the rationality of investor reaction. They conclude that investors are systematically misled by expectations management and cannot distinguish between firms that manage forecasts down and those that do not. Their findings suggest that downward (upward) forecast revisions cause investors to underestimate (overestimate) earnings resulting in positive (negative) abnormal returns upon the announcement of earnings. In support of Bernhardt and Campello's claim that investors are fooled by expectations management, Bartov et al.'s (2002) results suggest that firms that meet or beat forecasts through expectations management are associated with only a slightly lower premium than those that meet or beat forecasts via genuine means. Thus, market values are consistently greater for firms with positive earnings surprises even when the earnings target is achieved by dampening expectations (Kross, Ro, & Suk, 2011; Palmrose, Richardson, & Scholz, 2001).

Management's earnings forecasts choice might weaken its fiduciary responsibility to its stockholders since accurate reporting might not be management's single incentive in reporting a forecast. Previous research advocates that management's choices to report earnings guidance are linked to its self-interest (Matsumoto, 2002) and could indicate its incentive to influence the overall market response to earnings news (Baginski, Hassell, & Waymire, 1994; Bartov et al., 2002; Shivakumar, 2010; Zolotoy, Frederickson, & Lyon, 2012). This proof is in harmony with concerns that have been raised that manager's preannouncement choices are one of the earnings games managers consider with the purpose of avoiding reporting earnings lower than estimated earnings (Brown & Pinello, 2005; Campello, 2010; Cohen et al., 2011; Koch, Lefanowicz, & Shane, 2012). While the ethical literature identifies the ethically charged quality of earnings management (Arel, Beaudoin, & Cianci, 2011; Chen, Kelly, & Salterio, 2011; Kaplan & Ravenscroft, 2004; Merchant & Rockness, 1994), there has been less credit or knowledge of the ethical features of managements' guidance choices.

The next section will discuss the researches that consider the importance of meeting or beating forecasts.

2.7   Importance of Meeting or Beating Forecasts

Information in financial statements can facilitate investors' investment decisions. One of the most critical items in financial statements is earnings. Prior literature has investigated the information content of earnings at earnings announcement and established that earnings convey new information to the market. Ball and Brown (1968) conduct a seminal study that examines the role of earnings in the stock market and find a positive association between unexpected earnings and abnormal returns. The line of research that followed explored the relation between earnings and market reactions in terms of the magnitude of earnings surprises and examined whether the magnitude of earnings surprises varies across firm characteristics, such as earnings persistence, market risk, growth and so forth (Kormendi and Lipe, 1987; Easton and Zmijewski, 1989; Collins and Kothari, 1989). The underlying reasoning behind this line of research hinges on valuation models; that is, investors have expectations about firms' future performance and earnings surprises provide incremental information for investors to revise their beliefs. For example, if earnings surprise is positive, the investors may expect a firm to generate higher cash flows than they previously believed. In such case, the investors would revise their expectations on this firm's future cash flows upward, which results in a positive market response to this firm. On the other hand, if a firm announces lower earnings than the investors expected, the investors would lower their expectations about this firm's future cash flows. In such case, the market would react negatively to this firm. Indeed, the extant literature indicates that the sign of earnings surprise is an indication of firms' future performance. Bartov et al. (2002) provide evidence that firms that meet or beat expectations have higher growth in sales, return on equity and return on assets than firms that fall short of forecasts. Kasznik and McNichols (2002) show that future earnings are higher for firms that meet or beat forecasts than for firms that miss expectations. In addition, Feng (2004), using a signalling model, finds that firms that meet or marginally beat forecasts outperform firms that beat or miss forecasts by a larger margin in the future performance. She argues that this finding, given earnings management is costly to managers, is a result of managers' signalling their private information to the market by meeting or slightly beating expectations.

On the other hand, missing to meet the expectations could put the management in the danger of litigation. As a result, managers with bad earnings news tend to pre-disclose information to reduce the risk of litigation because it spreads the stock price shock over multiple dates (Skinner, 1994; (Kasznik & Lev, 1995)).

Consistent with this issue, Trueman (1997) indicates that good news information is expected to be more accurate than bad news information. He argued that bad news disclosures have both a constructive impact of lessening the likelihood of litigation and a undesirable effect of diminishing the company's share price, therefore the manager balances these effects by selecting an incorrect disclosure. However, since there are only positive consequences of good news, the manager favors full disclosure. Consistent with this rationale, Skinner (1994) indicates that bad news disclosures is likely to be qualitative whereas good news disclosures is likely to be point or range estimates. Since managers' forecast is a kind of information disclosure, both studies are in line with my hypotheses that bad news managers' forecasts are more pessimistically biased than their good news equivalents. Hurwitz (2001) contend that optimistic good news managers' forecasts entice litigations, but pessimism in bad news managers' forecasts assists in reducing rather than increasing litigation risk. As a result, managers may issue more credible (less optimistic) forecasts to reduce expected litigation costs and to restore investor confidence (Zhu, 2010).

2.8 Disadvantages of Forecasts Management

2.8.1 Managerial Opportunism and Managers' Earnings Forecasts

While Krehmeyer, Orsagh et al. (2006) and the related papers mainly concentrate on managers' earnings forecasts effect on myopia, the empirical literature has also considered whether managers utilize forecasts as a mean for self-improvement both via planned trading or influencing options prices. In general, literature proposes that there are concerns of managers' opportunism around managers' earnings forecasts. Insider trading likely represents the main capacity for managers' opportunism.

In relation to this, Penman (1982) indicates that managers plan their trades in the vicinity of forecasts in a way that is in accordance with trying to advantage from their insider information concerning the future disclosure. Utilizing larger samples with more recent data, researches have been capable to improve this awareness to indicate that management speculation is expected to happen through deliberately planning trades to follow managers' earnings forecasts and that managers are more expected to be engaged in buys that seem opportunistic than in opportunistic sales (Noe, 1999; Cheng and Lo, 2006).

Along with open trading in the market, some researches show that managers might use their power to plan when a forecast happens in a self-interested approach. Aboody and Kasznik (2000) find that bad news forecasts occurs before option award periods while good news forecasts are normally suspended until the award has happened. Apparently, such scheduling would raise the ultimate anticipated worth the option will give to the manager. In an analogous way, managers seem to boost the usage of good news forecasts if they are taking part in selling in a secondary stock offering, albeit there is no indication of raised use of managers' forecasts to assist secondary offerings in general (Frankel, McNichols and Wilson, 1995; Marquardt and Wiedman, 1998).

2.8.2   Fraud and Managers' Earnings Forecasts

The Krehmeyer, Orsagh et al.'s (2006) study and many observers highlight the likely role of extreme market expectations pushing managers on the way to committing counterfeit. These spectators mention that if such a relation be existent and if managers' earnings forecasts raise more attention on short term market prospects, then the forecasts might be part of the cause to these huge frauds. Several of these persons contend that the high costs of cheatings such as Enron or WorldCom basically eliminate any of the overall benefits from managers' earnings forecasts that were explained in the earlier sections of this chapter.

Unfortunately, the research findings can add a small amount of hard evidence to this discussion. These substantial deceptions are fairly uncommon in numbers. However, their huge costs leave such deceptions being crucial. In addition, every single fraud has exclusive features that make it unlike from previous frauds. Therefore, it is difficult to accumulate a large collection of data that affords clear study plan. Moreover, even after the event it is difficult to settle on what triggered a deception or even the real degree of the fraud.

For instance, although there were a lot of writings on Enron and much debate, the degree and roots are yet subject of dispute (see for example, Salter, 2008).

The best related big sample empirical evidence that can be considered is Kasznik (1999) which indicates that managers are expected to manipulate earnings (via accruals) with the intention of meeting the expectations determined in a managers' forecast of earnings.

Although these companies did not carry out the enormous aforementioned frauds, they definitely have attempted a slimy incline that is not advantageous for everyone included in the markets. All over again, there is the caution that these managers may be reacting to an ex-ante market attention on short term performance for their companies, and therefore would manipulate to some kind of target.

Further than scholar suggestion, one can also ponder the opposing claim that managers' earnings forecasts let managers to better manage expectations concerning their firm and therefore may help to decrease the stress to meet some outer market prospects. Literature earlier considered in this chapter indicates that managers can amend market expectations through the use of forecasts. This expectations adjustment presents an substitute to financial manipulation (Matsumoto, 2002).

In the next section, I explain the literature which relate to manipulative forecasts.

2.9 Manipulative Forecasts

In the opportunistic view in literature, managers deliberately manipulate forecasted and reported earnings. That is, managers intentionally conduct forecast management to misguide external stakeholders.

McGee, who is the head of quantitative research at Merrill Lynch, expresses the whole scenario through this short sentence in Wall street Journal "Investor-relations people have been making sure the hurdle of expectations remains low so their companies can clear it easily".[8]

The underlying issue that is also behind McGee's concern is that the management may prefer short-term profitability, as opposed to a long term one. Stein (2009) illustrates the idea that short-sighted managers care more about operation and the share prices of their business in the short-range, even at the cost of long-term profits. In addition, Stein (2009) states that due to their benefit agreements, managers tend to be less diversified, and a significant part of their revenue and wealth is frequently in the form of share and share options. Since they face liquidation requirements, they are more concerned about the company's stock price in the short range. Moreover, even when managers do not want to sell some of their shares in near future, managers' cash compensation, such as bonuses, in every period might be a function of the share price by the end of that period.

---

[8] McGee, S. 1997. As stock market surges ahead, 'predictable' profits are driving it. *Wall Street Journal*, May 5.

There have been some regulations to date that address these concerns. For example, Gong et al. (2003) states that one of the significant effects of Sarbanes Oxley (2002) (SOX), that was ratified after the scandals of Enron and WorldCom, was to limit the earning management of U.S. companies, with Bartov and Cohen (2009) mentioning that as a result of the SOX (2002) regulation, the intention to meet or beat analysts' expectations decreased in the post SOX period.

2.9.1 Managing Forecasts and Reported Earnings to Produce Positive Earnings Surprises

Despite the regulations that are imposed to limit manipulative disclosure, researchers express concerns over managers using their forecasts to strategically manage the analysts' consensus forecasts (Hochberg, Sapienza, & Rgensen, 2009). For instance, Frost (1989), Koch (2002) and Rogers and Buskirk (1997) claimed that Several stimulus elements is capable of inducing managers to intentionally tailor their prediction of earning to inflate market expectations. Also Graham et al. (2007) state that managers are worried about the stern market response for losing investors' and analysts' earnings anticipations, and are eager to make minor or moderate economic forgoes to meet those anticipations.

Similarly Brown & Caylor (2002) and Dechow et al. (2009) reported that since the mid-1990's, managers are generally worried about meeting or beating analysts' consensus earnings forecasts. Other Survey-based studies in Britain (Brown & Caylor, 2005) and the United States (Bundy, 2007) also show that meeting expectations is considered a fundamental target for the management. Cotter, Tuna, & Wysocki (2003) tries to clarify the management's attempt to meet the analysts' forecasts in a different way, by explaining that since the management try to manage the analysts' forecasts downward, bad-news forecasts are positively associated with the analysts' optimism.

On the other hand, Burgstahler and Dichev (1998) found that the management manipulate reported earnings in order to make a slight positive threshold. Degeorge, Patel and Zeckauser (1996) extend Burgstahler and Dichev (1998), finding both of the zero forecast error and previous year earnings as important benchmarks that the management wants to surpass. The analysts' consensus forecasts may be considered a target as well.

Similarly, since the charges of missing forecasts are expected to be higher for overrates than for underestimates, Kasznik (2006) and Xin (2012) stated that in order to avoid negative earnings surprises and consequent market's severe negative reactions, managers can manage earnings expectation downward, while managing reported earnings upward. They argued that in recent years, as a result of strict regulations, managers shifted from doing earnings management to doing expectation (forecast, guidance) management. In fact, recently, managers may use both income increasing earnings management or downward expectation management to avoid negative earnings surprises. The Kasznik finding is in contrast with Dutta and Gigler (2002), who state that through the collective roles of forecasts and earnings, more accurate information is effectively conveyed to the market.

Other studies also show that managers forgo long-term growth and long-term appreciation to avoid short-term negative earnings surprises (Cotter, Tuna, & Wysocki, 2006; Das et al., 2008; Kasznik, 1999a). This is consistent with the anecdotes that managers are aware of the analysts' expectations, and sometimes go out of their way to avoid missing benchmarks (Sun & Xu, 2012).

More recently, Bennett & Bradbury (2001) found that companies that are right above the benchmarks have normal receivables, inventories and provisions. However, they increase cash from customers and decrease inventories. Other studies (Payne & Robb, 2000) highlighted the fact that the management manipulates earning to reduce their forecast error in the earnings announcement date. Finally, they concluded that in companies with irregular cash flows, the stock price is highly sensitive to their forecasted earnings, and the management tend to reveal the forecast for such companies, and consequently reduce forecast error through earnings management (Payne & Robb, 2000).

Other researchers suggest that companies engage in real actions to meet the benchmarks (Bennett & Bradbury, 2010; Beyer, 2009; Brown, 2001; Bundy, 2007). Barua et al. (2006) stating that the tendency to meet a benchmark in a profitable or non-profitable company is the result of different accruals of management activities. Similarly, Das, Kim and Patro (1997) found that the Expectation management has an important impact on the earnings management, but the opposite does not hold. That is, there is recursive relationship between the expectation management and earnings management. Moreover, Dutta and Gigler (2002) showed that the management generally tends to manage earnings to meet expectations, and will particularly tend to manage earnings with regards to their forecasts.

2.9.2 Forecasts Management Instead of Earnings Management

Certain researchers place emphasis on the forecast management, rather than on earnings management. For example, Kross et al. (2011), suggest that ''meet or beat'' firms are more likely to issue bad news forecasts. In addition, Dechow et al. (2009), Coulton et al. (2006), Beaver et al. (2005) and Durtschi & Easton (2005) doubted whether the experienced kink in the distribution of earnings is solely caused by earnings management.

They further state that forecast management could also be used along with earnings management.

For example, Gong et al. (2003) indicated that when the mandatory (such as accrual reporting) and voluntary (such as management earnings forecast) reporting of a manager are under the influence of the management's subjectivity, similar to the mandatory reported information, voluntarily disclosed information may contain bias, and such biases will potentially reduce the value of the information of voluntary disclosure.

Similar to Gong et al. (2003), (Beaver, McNichols, & Nelson, 2006) finds that the management's forecast contains significant error in relation to historical return of the stock. They suggest that the management cannot incorporate information about past stock prices into their forecasts. However, Hirst et al. (2012) consider stock prices as an antecedent of forecast management. They believe that stock prices influence the management's incentive towards issuing a forecast. Managers with strong incentives tied to the firm's stock price (a forecast antecedent) are viewed as issuing self-serving forecasts (Correia, Flynn, Uliana, & Wormald, 2010). However, various levels of managerial incentives, such as equity-based compensation, occur through firms and time. Specially, equity-based compensation accounted for less than 20% of a CEO's compensation in 1980, but rose to nearly 50% by 1994 (Durtschi & Easton, 2005), and grew even higher to nearly 60% by 2003 (Beaver et al., 2006).

Consistent with Beyer's (1998) finding that the stock market is, on average, more susceptible to reported earnings than to the analyst's forecasts, Bergman & Roychowdhury (2005), Cotter et al. (2003) and Matsumoto (2008) argue that the recent fad in forecast pessimism is frequently explained as the result of the management's wish to use their earnings forecasts as a way to walk-down market earnings prospects. Managers purposely report pessimistic forecasts that, in turn, cause market participants to dial down their expectations. Even though this behaviour generates bad-news from the managers' forecasts, it later produces an simpler benchmark to meet or beat when the actual earnings are reported (Hirst et al., 2008). Such a view is more consistent with opportunism than to informative forecasts, because in this view, the management's forecast does not convey the management's true expectation to the market. Bergman and Roychowdhury (2005) finds that for short-range forecasts that are optimistic in nature, managers incline to walk-down analyst forecasts to realized earnings. The next section presents the theories that are behind the opportunistic perspective.

2.9.3 Theoretical Arguments: Producing Positive Earnings Surprise

As mentioned earlier in section 1.1, the Positive Accounting Theory assumes that all actions by all individuals, including the management (as agent), are driven by self-interest. Since the management's compensation is either in the form of cash bonus on any increases in the share price, options, or shares in the firm (Farrell, 2005), the increase in stock prices is in the management's best interest. According to the prospect theory and transaction cost theory, the management increase stock prices by beating expectations. This phenomenon is best illustrated by explaining the prospect theory and transaction cost theory in the next two sections.

2.9.3.1 *Prospect Theory*

According to Kahneman and Tversky (2007), the prospect theory assumes that decision-makers stem value from gains and losses with regard to wealth reference points, rather than from certain levels of wealth. The Prospect theory can be used to justify why managers produce downward biased forecasts to create positive earnings surprises. The reason is that investors compare the reported earnings to a reference point, and that reference point could easily be the earnings forecasts.

In addition, the prospect theory suggests that the individuals' value functions are concave in profits and convex in losses (S-shaped). In other words, the value functions are sharpest around the wealth's reference points (Burgstahler & Dichev, 1997). Making the earnings forecasts as reference points will clearly demonstrate why it is important for managers to actually reach forecasts. This is because the value of the function is steepest around the forecasts. Therefore, for a given rise in wealth, the related growth in value is highest when the rise in wealth moves the individual from a loss to a gain, in relation to the reference point.

The Prospect theory has been confirmed by several empirical studies in the field of forecasts management. For example, Rogers and Stocken (2010) found that the market behaves as if good news are less credible than bad news. Similarly, Williams (2002) argues that good news forecasts are not as reliable as bad news forecasts. Hutton et al. (2003) also contend that bad news forecasts are fundamentally more realistic than good news forecasts.

Keeping in mind that investors consider bad news from negative earnings surprise as credible and consequently adjust the stock price downward, the management of both buy and sell companies prefer to avoid negative earnings surprises. This is consistent with Burgstahler and Dichev's (1997) argument on managerial opportunistic behaviour theory, which is about the motivation to the manager in avoiding income decreases or losses. Consistent with this theory, Burgstahler & Dichev (1997) reported that the management uses cash flow from operations and fluctuations in working capital to accomplish the manipulation of earnings and avoid negative earnings surprises. This is consistent with the assumptions of the transaction cost theory, which will be explained in the next section, when investors use heuristics to determine terms of transaction with the firms; by avoiding negative earnings surprises, the companies will face lower costs when transacting with stakeholders.

2.9.3.2 *Transaction Cost Theory*

The expectation for the behaviour of the companies to meet forecasts (esp. sell companies) is consistent with the assumptions of the transaction cost theory, where it attempts to justify why firms exist, and why they enlarge or outsource certain operations. The transaction cost theory assumes that firms attempt to decrease the costs of trading capitals with the surroundings, and that firms also try to minimize the administrative costs of exchanges internally. Firms are hence balancing the costs of trading capitals with the surroundings compared to the administrative costs of performing operations internally.

The theory perceives organizations and marketplace as diverse potential forms of forming and managing economic dealings. When the external contract costs are greater than the firm's internal administrative expenses, the firm will expand, as the company is able to do its actions at lower costs, than if the operations were done in the market. Conversely, if the administrative expenses for organizing the action are greater than the exterior operation costs, the firm will be downscaled. According to Ronald Coase (1979), every firm will enlarge provided that the firm's operations can be done at lower cost in-house, than by e.g. contract out the operations to outside suppliers in the market.

According to Williamson (1996), a transaction cost occurs "when a good or a service is transferred across a technologically separable interface". Thus, the transaction costs occur whenever a service or product is being moved from one phase to another, where new groups of technical skills are required to create a service or product. Thus, if firms perceive the high environmental insecurity, they might select not to outsource or interchange capitals with the surroundings.

The Transaction cost theory is built on the next two postulations (Burgstahler & Dichev, 1997).

The first assumption is that companies with greater incomes incure lower costs in transactions with stakeholders (Burgstahler & Dichev, 1997). Cornell and Shapiro (1937) suggest that the worth of stakeholders' inherent rights (which is exactly connected with the market value of the company) is susceptible to the news regarding the company's financial situation. More explicitly, Bowen et al. (1981), discusses motivations to report greater earnings with regard to customers, employees, lenders, suppliers, and other stakeholders. Examples of encouragements to report greater profits include customers who are eager to give a better price for goods as the company is expected to award inherent guarantee and service obligations. Suppliers propose finer conditions, since the company is more probable to pay for present buys and likewise since the company is more expected to have greater upcoming buys. Creditors will suggest superior conditions since the company is less probable to either avoid or postpone loan payments. Moreover, precious staffs are less probable either to leave or to request higher wages in order to stay.

The second notion is that interested parties use heuristics to decide the conditions of dealings with the company. The use of heuristics rises as a reaction to information costs in financial models (Cornell & Shapiro, 1987). When it is expensive for stakeholders to process complete information concerning incomes for all of the companies with which they cope with implicitly and explicitly, some stakeholders use heuristic cut-offs like earnings forecasts. Although the focus for such information processing heuristic theory is on the stakeholders, since the stakeholders focus on reported earning, forecasts and stock price to form their expectation for companies' future profitability and growth, this provides enough incentives for the management to create positive forecast error and increase stock prices. Consistently, Matsumoto (2008) state that as easily accessible from several sources (e.g., First Call, Zacks, I/B/E/S), earnings surprises are a straightforward, valid heuristic on which to found trades, and institutional investors are expected to respond sturdily to negative earnings surprises. The fact that the management of both buy and sell companies like to have positive forecast errors is in line with the information processing heuristic theory. Therefore, earnings forecasts are considered as important benchmarks for managers.

2.9.4 The use of Prospect Theory and Transaction Cost Theory to Explain Management Incentive to Produce Positive Earnings Surprises

Applying prospect theory to the investors' task of judging firm value, the earnings expectation immediately preceding receipt of an earnings signal is the relevant reference point (Pinello, 2004). For example, the relevant reference point when evaluating a revised forecast would be the earnings expectation immediately prior to receipt of that revised forecast (i.e., the initial forecast). By contrast, the relevant reference point when evaluating actual earnings would be the most recent expectation (i.e., the revised forecast).

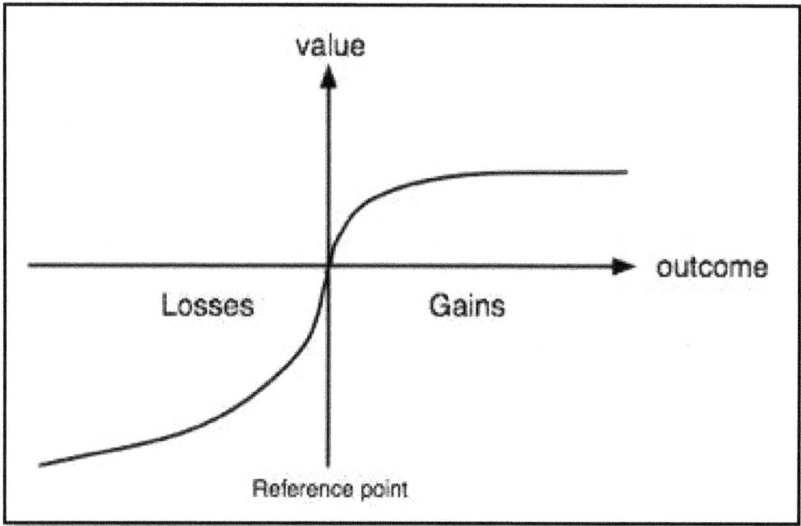

Figure 2-1. Individual value function.
Individual Value function is concave in gains and convex in losses and steepest around wealth reference point (Burgstahler and Dichev, 1997, Kahneman & Tversky, 1979).

The characteristics of the value and weighting functions are predictive of certain judgmental effects. As shown in Figure 2-1, the value function is concave beyond the reference point and convex under the reference point resulting in an S-shaped curve reflective of diminishing sensitivity. Diminishing sensitivity implies that the marginal value of deviations from the reference point decreases with the magnitude of the deviation. As described by Thaler (Thaler, 2004), both the gain and loss functions reflect diminishing sensitivity such that the difference between $10 and

$20 seems bigger than the difference between $1000 and $1010, regardless of the sign of the difference. In addition, the loss function is steeper than the gain function, reflecting individuals' tendency to be loss averse. Individuals are loss averse because their dislike for losses exceeds their like for equivalent gains. Losing $10 yields more displeasure than gaining $10 yields pleasure.

2.10 Forecasts Management Decreases Information Asymmetry (Efficiency Perspective)

In contrast to the view that managers deliberately manipulate forecasted and reported earnings and intentionally conduct forecast management to misguide external stakeholders, there is an informative view in literature in which managers' issue forecasts to alleviate information asymmetry.

In the informative view of forecasts management, management will manage earnings in order to reduce information asymmetry. In fact, by doing so, the management discloses more information to the external stakeholders. Hui, Matsunaga and Morse (1983) state that using forecasts as a voluntary information disclosure tool is an important component of the firms informational environment.

Likewise, Hirst, Koonce, and Venkataraman (2012) proposed that since management earnings forecasts passes the manager's insider information to the stockholders, it reduces the information asymmetry and precludes costly stockholder litigation against the firm. Therefore, it increases the firm's stature as a disclosure of transparent information (Irani & Karamanou, 2003). Further, Dutta and Gigler (2002) state that in previous theories of earnings management, the reported earnings were modelled in such a way that it was perceived as a message from the management to communicate the true earnings to the shareholders in the principal agent context.

In addition, Lennox and Park (1995) argue that the managers theoretically use earnings forecast to reduce information asymmetry. Other studies also showed that the managers' forecast reduces the information asymmetry either between the manager and the investors, or between different groups of investors. For instance, Ajinkya and Gift (2005) found that the management predicts earnings with the purpose of manoeuvring the investors' expectation about future profits towards management's belief.

Kasznik and Lev (1995) used the degree of earning surprise as a gauge for information symmetry. They found that when negative earnings surprise is larger, it is more likely that managers predict bad news. However, he found no relation between positive earnings surprises and managers' forecasting of good news. Consistent with Kasznik and Lev's result, Hui, Matsunaga and Morse (1983) concur that since managers' forecasts can replace conservatism, such a replacement can be considered as a sign of usefulness to managers' forecasts. They interpreted their result as managers transferring information to the stockholders either by conservatism, or by managers' forecast. Similarly Hui et al. (2009) documented that accounting conservatism acts as a substitute for management earnings forecasts. However, in their recent study by differentiating between informative and non-informative forecasts, Jaggi and Xin (2006) found that conservatism serves as a substitute only for informative management earnings forecasts that reduce information asymmetry and not for non-informative forecasts that do not reduce information asymmetry.

Clarkson, Dontoh, Richardson and Sefcik (1995) and Jog and McConomy (2012) investigated why some Canadian companies that have Initial Public Offerings (IPO) forecast future earnings in their prospectuses, while others do not. Their results showed that voluntary forecast is a sign of good news, and is conveyed as such to the participants. Voluntary forecasts, that includes managers' forecast has an important effect on information asymmetry.

2.10.1 Relationship of Forecasts and Future Earnings Management

Some researchers regard issuing forecasts as restricting management to be incapable of conducting earnings management. For example, Dutta and Gigler (2002) showed that, if the management is asked to make a forecast, it will inadvertently hamper their ability to conduct earnings management. They argue that because of the collective roles that forecasts, along with manipulated reported earnings play in conveying extra information on management expectation to stockholders, it might not be in the best interest of the stockholders to restrict earnings management. In addition, Dutta and Gigler (2002) show that issuing forecasts has endogenous benefits to stockholders in restricting earnings management, and there is an endogenous cost for the manager to miss the forecasts. Finally Dutta and Gigler (2002) propose an optimal contractual based framework, in which the forecast causes restriction on earnings management, there is an endogenous benefit of voluntary forecast for shareholders. Furthermore, in that framework, there are endogenous costs for managers for not reacting to forecasts.

In contrast to Dutta and Gigler (2002) that shows forecasts and consequent earnings management having a collective role of conveying extra information on management expectation to investors, Athanasakou, Strong and Walker (1992) found that there is no positive relation between abnormal income increasing working capital accruals and the probability of meeting or beating the analyst's forecasts. That is, the management do not manipulate earnings to concur with previously forecasted profit. The finding that there is no relationship between forecasts and earnings management contradicts Dutta and Gigler's proposition that forecasts and earnings management plays a collective role in conveying management expectation to the investors.

Lennox and Park (2006), Pinello (2004), Hurwitz (2012) and Hirst et al, (2008) highlighted that by issuing forecast, the management reduces information asymmetry. However, after issuing forecasts, the extent to which the management uses accruals to convey its subjective information to shareholders is under the effect of the nature of activity, the type of industry and available accounting choices under Generally Accepted Accounting Principles (GAAP) (Irani & Karamanou, 2003). Finally, Diamond and Verrecchia (2003), Lennox & Park (2006) and (Pinello, 2004) stated that the reduction in information asymmetry will lead to an increase in liquidity and the reduction of the cost of the capital (Lennox and Park 2006). The next section presents the theories that support this view.

2.10.2 Efficiency Perspective (Theoretical support)

2.10.2.1 *Expectation Adjustment Hypothesis*

After explaining the theories that justify the behaviour of sell companies, I now turn to the theories that justify the behaviour of buy companies. Firm managers forecast earnings for several reasons: The "expectations adjustment hypothesis" posits that managers issue forecasts in order to align the investors' beliefs with their own (Graham et al., 2005; Hassell & Jennings, 1986).

This is the underlying theory of benevolent (truthful) forecasts. Managers may also forecast to decrease information asymmetry in the market (Athanasakou, Strong, & Walker, 2009). While the management's ability to forecast accurately is a function of the quality of the firm's information systems, their willingness to align investor expectations more closely with their own depends on the management's incentives to forecast accurately (Hutton & Stocken, 2009). This shows that the management's incentive is imperative in forecast accuracy.

Presuming that the management pursues to line up market expectations with their own expectations (see Ajinkya & Gift, 1984), it is precisely correct when the management conveys extreme news. A favourable forecasting reputation results from a favourable track record, which is most helpful for enhancing forecast credibility, and as it will be explained later in the next chapter, the buy companies are supposed to be the companies that have strong financial position and high expected future growth, and I hypothesize that the expectation adjustment hypothesis is true for buy companies, making it consistent with the revelation principle.

2.10.2.2 *Revelation Principle*

The Revelation principle posits that any likely balanced result of any viable mechanism, however complicated, can be reproduced by a truth-expressive equilibrium result of a system under which the agents are inquired to state their private information (Hirst et al., 2008). In other words, once the revelation principle is valid, any equilibrium that contains on-truthful reporting (namely one in which opportunistic forecasts management is taking place) can always be weakly dominated by one where truth telling is induced (Beyer et al., 2010).

The Revelation principle was first introduced by Gibbard (1991) and were later expanded by Dasgupta, Hammond and Maskin (1990), Holmstrom (1973), and Myerson (1979). The revelation principle, which states that there is no loss of generality in restricting the analysis to truth telling and full disclosure equilibrium, was invoked to address asymmetric information, in which the truth is instrumental in the implementation of efficient allocation (Gibbard, 1973; Holmstrom, 1977).

Based on the revelation principle, for any principle agent model, any equilibrium of a rational communication strategy for economic agents can be simulated by an equivalent incentive-compatible direct-revelation mechanism. In other words, the revelation principle states that any equilibrium outcome of any mechanism, however complex, can be replicated by a truth-telling equilibrium outcome of a mechanism under which the agents are asked to report their private information to the principal (see, for example, Myerson (1979)). Hence, when the revelation principle holds, the performance of any mechanism under which managers engage in manipulated reporting can be replicated by a mechanism under which the managers will report truthfully.

Based on this principle, in the agent-principle model of the firm, in order for a rational communication strategy to be stimulated for an agent, the management, acting as an agent, should reveal the correct private information to the market. Dye (1988, page 200) observes that "when the manager can communicate all dimensions of his private information to the shareholders, the Revelation Principle does indeed apply, and so no internal demand exists for manipulative reporting."

The revelation principle's assumptions are related to communication, the contract form, and commitment. It assumes that communication is not blocked (it is costless to establish communication channels that allow the agents to fully report their private information), the form of the contract is not restricted, and the principal can commit to use the reports submitted by the agents in any pre-specified manner.

Interestingly, many researchers that have focused on inaccurate reporting have started to build models that guarantee the revelation principle does not hold. Although this does not ensure the non-truthful equilibrium will be optimal, it will at least open the possibility.

However, literature on earnings and forecasts management show that there are violation to the assumptions of the revelation principle. There have been three distinct approaches where researchers have combined elements intended to evade the revelation principle. Some of these violations and their consequences are elaborated in the subsequent sections.

The most straightforward way to circumvent the revelation principle is to exogenously limit the agent's capability to convey their information. On the other hand, several models set limitations on the principal's ability to utilize the information, such as by needing the principal utilize an agreement with a pre-defined form (for instance, piece-wise linear). Lastly, the researchers have loosened the assumption that there is pre-obligation as to in what way the agent's report will be utilized. These three ways of violation of the revelation principles are explained in the following paragraphs.

Inability of the agent to communicate well - Communication limits and costs may link either to the restrictions on the manager's ability to provide, or restriction on the ability of the manager to properly convey their information. When any sort of communication constraint exists, it is likely that non-truthful reporting occurs (Beyer et al., 2010). The violation of the communication assumptions will also occur if there are immediate costs of reporting the "truth". For instance, assume the "unmanaged" earnings number includes noises that the manager can perceive. However, it is expensive to take measures to eliminate the noises. The principal can only perceive the final report, but not the initial earnings number, or whether the manager has interfered to remove the noise (Beyer et al., 2010). Verrecchia (1986) indicates that it is advantageous to allow the managers themselves choose when to eliminate the noises. Essentially, it is very expensive for the principal to persuade the manager to continually suffer the cost of noise removal.

The other kind of communication constraint is that the agent cannot completely convey the rich dimensions of their information. Managers often see very rich information sets that would be extremely hard and expensive to convey. Furthermore, the principal will usually not have the specialized capability to realize various aspects of the agent's information set. When these kinds of constraints exist on the manager's ability to provide information, the revelation principle fades almost by definition. Now, the reporting problem contains an aggregation dimension as well as a misstatement dimension.

Dye (1988), Evans and Sridhar (2009), and Demski (1998) emphasis on settings in which the Revelation Principle does not hold because the agent is unable to fully communicate their private information.

According to Abarbanell and Lehavy (2003b) sell companies face constraints in manipulation of the profit as they don't seem to have new markets and high potential return. In addition the sell company's stock price sensitivity to earnings news is not high. Such commitments limit the sell companies to communicate the full dimensions of their information set to the market. Therefore, as shown in Dutta and Gigler (2002), and Abarbanell and Lehavy (2003b), due to the limitations of the resources that the sell companies have, they suffer from communication constraints. The limitations of the resources come in the form of a lack of new products, new markets, and the lack of lucrative investment opportunities. This is most logical as the lack of resources will render the sell companies unable to communicate the full dimensionality of their rich information set to investors through the manipulation of reported earnings. For this reason, sell companies are expected to have different approaches in transmission of information to investors compared to buy companies.

Inability to pre-commit to how the information is used - The pre-obligation assumption is vital to the revelation principle due to the principal's assurance of "under-utilize" the information is what gives the agent a motivation to disclose the reality. If an agent deems the information will be exploited against them, it turns out to be more expensive (may be too costly) to motivate them to disclose the reality. One approach in which the pre-commitment assumption has been loosened is by presuming there are other groups who refer tithe agent's report who cannot pre-commit on how they will actually exploit it. For instance, this third party could be an auditor who is appointed to give an opinion regarding the agent and his reports. Baiman et al. (1987) analysed a model, in which they showed that the equilibrium could not be achieved if the agent permanently tells the reality and for the auditor to work hard to examine the agent's report. In other words, if the auditor is persuaded the agent's report is reliable; he has no motivation to waste time and money to do auditing. In theory, the third party could also be another employee of the firm, arrival, the labour market (in setting the value of the agent's outside employment opportunities in the future) or even the stock market (in setting the value of the agent's stock-based compensation), and the revelation principle would not be relevant in this case.

As some examples of violation of the pre-commitment assumption, Demski and Frimor (1979), and Christensen, Demski, and Frimor (2002) examine the models in which the Revelation Principle fails due tithe principal's inability to commit.

On the other hand, Arya et al. (2008) states that the principal is unable to make long-term commitments. Therefore, the principal engages in ex-post opportunistic actions that are detrimental from an ex-ante perspective. In such settings, the earning management is beneficial as it restricts the amount of information that the principal receives at the renegotiation stage. When the communication between the management and the investor is merely based on reported earnings, and since the principal finds it desirable to induce earnings management to discipline their ex-post opportunistic behaviour, the revelation principle applies. Furthermore, as I will explain in section 3.11, Dutta and Gigler (2003) mentioned that if the communication is based on both reported earnings and forecast of future earnings, the principal can make commitments and their communication is unrestricted. Therefore, earnings management can be beneficial as it reduces the cost of eliciting truthful forecasts from the manager.

Restricted Contract Form – The violation of the revelation principle may also happen when the researcher exogenously limits the structure of the compensation contract. For example, Demski and Dye (1999) analysed a one-period example, in which the agent is accountable for events that shape both the mean and the variance of the end-of-period cash flows. At the beginning of the period, the agent observes private information regarding the mean and the variance, and s/he discloses both of these parameters to the principal. Nevertheless, the contract is constrained to a linear function of the end-of-period cash flow, with a penalty term that is proportionate to the square of the deviation of the recognized cash flow from the forecasted mean. They clearly showed that the manager's report continually undervalues the estimated cash flow. That is, in their model, the manager attempts to build slack into his forecast. On the other hand, the reporting models that employ optimal contracts such as Antle and Fellingham (1997) or Kirby et al. (1991), the manager's forecast is unprejudiced, and it is the principal who gives the slack to the agent as an inducement for the agent to provide an honest forecast.

Demski and Frimor (1999) indicate that the revelation principle can be circumvented; however, the principal can create a plausible two-period contract, supposing that the principal and agent can renegotiate their stipulations in the second period. In these models, the agent predicts that the principal will use their report against them afterwards, and this makes reporting the truth extremely costly for the agent involved.

Whereas exogenously stipulating the form of the contract can be useful in understanding the reporting motivations entailed in that structure, it asks for the question of why the compensation is structured in such as way. Currently, I have especially trivial knowledge as to why the compensation contracts have the form they do, why the elements are piece-wise linear, or why bonuses are "lumpy", i.e., the highest bonus is paid if the performance surpasses a level, and no bonus at all is paid albeit the performance barely misses this threshold. Occasional empiricism proposes that contracts with these features are very widespread, and that these elements have an important effect on the managers' motivations. The linear contracting framework is unable of giving understandings into these matters; and a more common (ideally, an optimal) contracting framework is necessary. Dutta and Gigler (2002) suggest a new contractual model in which the management utility is mainly based on whether the reported earning meet or miss the forecasts.

2.10.2.2.1 **Relationship of Truth Telling and Revelation Principle**

The existence of truth telling mechanisms is not the same as stating that the revelation principle holds. In order to emphasize this point, if the revelation principle holds, then there are mechanisms for eliciting the truth, yet the existence of these mechanisms does not mean that the revelation principle will actually hold. What I am trying to show is that there is a scope for forecasts management inside games, where the truth revealing equilibrium can be shown to exist using standard mechanisms associated with the revelation principle. In this research, like of Ronen and Yaari (1979), the revelation principles holds in a sub-game but probably fails to hold in the complete game. On the other hand, the revelation principle states that there is no loss of generality in restricting the analysis to a game in which the arbitrator designs an incentive-compatible mechanism (a mechanism that elicits full, truth telling messages). The intuition is that the arbitrator can induce the privately formed players to fully report the truth (Dasgupta et al., 1979).

As Dye writes, the revelation principal is "a nemesis to the study of opportunistic reporting". This is because economic explanations for opportunistic reporting require one or more of the assumptions of the revelation principle to be explicitly violated (Dye, 1988).

Consistent with Dutta and Gigler's (2002) model, which is explained in the next section, the revelation principle might be true for buy and sell companies. The reason is that, for buy companies, the forecasts convey the management's true expectation to the market that is followed by income increasing earnings management. However, for the Sell companies, the forecasts do not convey true (or optimistic) information to the market, but, it is used to dampen the market expectation so that the management can benefit from a positive stock price shock, which is the result of positive earnings surprise.

In this section, two opposing views of Earnings and forecasts management were proposed. These views are informative versus delusive earnings and forecasts management. As Hirst et al. (2012) confirmed, interaction tests are probably useful in reconciling contrasting views in the literature. Including a theoretically motivated conditioning, or moderator, variable in the relationship between forecasts and earnings management will often allow the researchers to identify where the effect holds or where it does not (or where it holds in a different way).

2.11 Model Suggested by Dutta and Gigler (2002)

Dutta and Gigler (2002) provide a theoretical model that explains and integrate both pessimistic (opportunistic) and optimistic (efficiency) forecasts behaviour of companies. Dutta & Gigler (2002) theoretical model is about the effect of earnings forecasts on earnings management, and the implication of their model to this work is explained as follows.

Dutta & Gigler (2002) define at least two types of earnings, economic and accounting earnings. Economic earnings is the real increase in the value of the company while Accounting earning is the earning that is reported in the financial statements. They suggest that since reported accounting earnings are not the same as the true economic earnings, the management tries to convey additional information about true economic earning to the market via forecasts.

They assume two types of firm's outputs. One is high output and the other is low output. Firm's output $=x$ and $x \epsilon \{x_L, x_H\}$

Assuming that both predicted and reported earnings influence the management's compensation, they develop the following framework.

They consider $s(\hat{x}, y)$ as denoting the manager's compensation in the state when they issue forecast $\hat{x}$ and realized accounting earning is y. For U_{ij} is used to denote $U(s(\hat{x}_i, y_i))$, where U represents management's utility.

In the presence of forecasts, Dutta and Gigler (2002) propose optimal communication contracts, in which the managers who report low economic earnings are shielded from the risk associated with the accounting earnings. That is, the optimal communication contract sets $U_{\hat{L}H}$ equal to $U_{\hat{L}L}$. On the other hand, the optimal contract penalizes a manager who reports a high economic income when such a report is followed by low accounting income (i.e. $U_{\hat{H}H} > U_{\hat{H}L}$). This penalty must be sufficiently large to ensure that the low type manager (i.e., the manager who observes $x = x_L$) does not mimic the high type (i.e., the manager who observes $x = x_H$), by issuing a high forecast and subsequently manipulating earnings. On the other hand, this penalty cannot be too large; otherwise the high type manager will have incentives to engage in earnings manipulation.

According to Dutta and Gigler (2002) in optimal communication contract:

$$U_{\hat{H}H} > U_{\hat{H}L} \qquad\qquad (2\text{-}-1)$$

$$U_{\hat{L}H} = U_{\hat{L}L} \qquad\qquad (2\text{-}-2)$$

The proposition stated in equations 2-1 and 2-2 is used as the bases of theoretical framework in the hypothesis development section.

To see how Dutta and Gigler's (2002) proposition is used as a basis for my theoretical framework, I should first consider the communication restriction that exists for sell companies (assumption of revelation principle does not hold). The reason is that according to Abarbanell and Lehavy (2003b); first, due to the lack of resources, sell companies cannot conduct earnings management and consequently, will not convey insider information to the market via doing earnings management and second, even if they conduct earnings management due to low stock price sensitivity to earnings news (Demski & Frimor, 1999) of sell companies', they cannot significantly increase the stock price through earnings manipulation. Therefore, sell companies cannot efficiently manage earnings and communication restrictions binds them. On the other hand, issuing high forecasts help the buy companies in the process of their financial reporting, because according to equation 2-1 and 2-2, having issued high forecasts, they can efficiently manage earnings to meet those forecasts ($U_{\hat{H}H}$). Issuing high forecasts however, does not help the sell companies in the process of their financial reporting, because considering market punishment that results from missing forecasts (equations 2-1 and 2-2), and since they cannot efficiently manage earnings, they will inevitably issue low forecasts.

This view of Dutta and Gigler (2002) is implicitly consistent with several empirical researches. For example, consistent with Dutta and Gigler (2002), Barua et al. (2006) confirms that before the accrual management for the companies that generated profit, compared to the companies that experienced loss, it was more likely that their pre-managed earning are less than both analysts' forecast and prior period's earning, and it is also more likely for them to report profits above the benchmarks.

Equation 2-2 (on page 85) is also consistent with Matsumoto's (2008) belief that the managers are likely concerned that a negative earnings surprise will lead to significantly lower stock prices, and adversely affect their performance evaluation. Similarly, Puffer and Weintrop (2003) find that the probability of a CEO's turnover increases with the shortfall of actual earnings from the analysts' expectations.

The next sections will discuss different views of growth and non-growth firms.

2.12 Different Views of Growth and Non-growth Firms

Previous studies suggested that various incentive elements can motivate managers to tailor their forecasts to inflate market expectations (Frost, 1997; Fuller & Jensen, 2002; Stein, 1989). For example, Frost (1989) investigated the disclosure policies of UK firms whose audit reports where modified. He illustrated that the disclosure statements of the firms that are under stress are often not credible, and the market usually discounts them. Similarly, Koch (2002) examined the relation between financial distress, bias in managers' forecasts, and the credibility of voluntary managers' forecasts. His findings show that in companies that are financially distressed, the managers' forecasts are biased, and are less credible than firms that are not financially distressed. Similarly, Rogers & Stocken (2010) examine the association of financial distress with managers' forecast bias, and discovered that distressed firms are generally more biased in their forecasts.

Stein (2009) mentions that the disappointing results that selling companies usually deals with increase the risk of termination of the management's contract, and that might be the possible reason for doing earnings and forecasts management. In addition, facing the possibility of a takeover increases the managers' interest in the short-term stock prices (Linck et al., 2009). Other researches also show that litigation risk does indeed influence issuing forecasts. For instance, Cao and

Narayanamoorthy (2005) finds that when faced with high ex-ante litigation risk, managers of firms with bad news are more likely to issue earnings guidance. However, regardless of ex-ante litigation risk, managers with good news are least likely to issue earnings guidance.

Brown, et al. (2005) discovered that a higher litigation risk is associated with more forecasts by both good-news and bad news firms. After controlling for litigation risk, however, they find that bad-news firms are significantly more likely to issue a forecast relative to good-news firms. This finding is consistent with Kasznik and Lev (1995), who also discovered that bad-news firms are significantly more likely to issue warnings relative to good-news firms.

In addition, poor performing management is likely to deal with stock price decline, and as a result, board of directors and investors put tremendous pressure on them (Puffer & Weintrop, 1991). Under such circumstance, the management faces a high contract termination risk. For instance, DeAngelo (1988) suggests that poor earnings performance is an obvious signal of management inefficiency. It can weaken the stockholders support and culminates in the termination of the management job itself. Similarly, Weisbach (2007) documents that stock returns and earnings changes is a reliable indicator of a CEO's resignation.

Warner et al. (1988) also finds an inverse relation between the stock performance and the probability of a management change.

Consequently, in order to alleviate the pressure from investors and the board of directors, and to mitigate the higher turnover risk when information indicating poor performance is released, managers may engage in producing downward biased forecast and income increasing earnings management to create positive earnings surprises. This is consistent with results documented by Frankel, McNichols and Wilson (1988), who found that firms seeking more external financing tend to issue managers' forecasts more frequently, and Miller (1988), who discovered that, companies that have a higher probability of growth are more likely to disclose their information to the market. Similarly, Ajinkya et al. (1995), and Rogers & Stocken (2010), claim that managers of firms with higher growth opportunities may be more optimistic about the future prospects of their company. However, non-growth firms are not optimistic about future prospects of their companies. This notion makes us expect that sell companies, which are usually non-growth companies (Abarbanell and Lehavy 2003b), are pessimistic about the future prospects of their companies, and will issue pessimistic forecasts.

Overall, it is established that documented market characteristics of stocks and the status of a company's profitability provides enough incentives for its management to conduct earnings management and forecasts management.

Figure 2-2 depicts the conceptual model of the study.

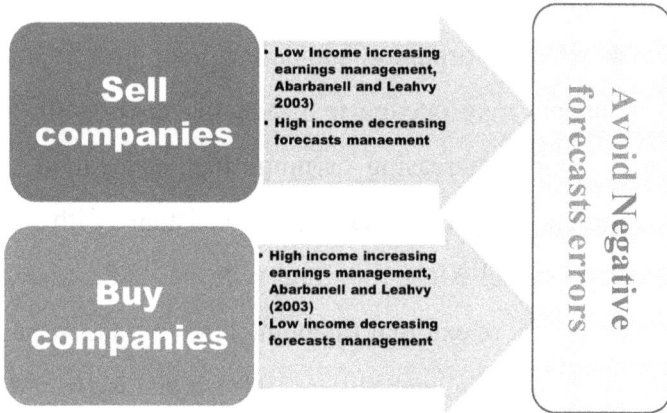

Figure 2-2. Conceptual model of the study.

As it is shown in the Figure 2-2, the sell companies are expected to reveal pessimistic forecasts and therefore the reported (issued) forecasts should be lower than their unmanaged (real) forecasts[9]. On the other hand, the buy companies are expected to issue optimistic forecasts and therefore their unbiased forecasts are expected to be lower than their issued forecasts. In addition both

---

[9]Following (Liu & Natarajan, 2012)"unmanaged" forecast refers to a forecast made by a rational manager who is an efficient information processor and does not indulge in strategic behaviour.

of the buy and sell group companies are expected to have positive forecasts errors.

2.13 Summary

In a nutshell, this chapter explained empirical findings with regards to two different views about optimistic and pessimistic forecasts that are in the literature. It is extensively shown using Duta and Gigler's (2002) framework, it is expected that consistent with the expectation adjustment hypothesis and in the context that revelation principle holds, through the issuing of optimistic forecasts, buy companies try to convey information to outsiders. However, in the sell companies, since they do not possess sufficient resources to convey information through manipulation of the reported earnings and consistent with Dutta and Gigler's framework, in order to avoid undesirable consequences of big negative earnings surprises in terms of litigation and loss of reputation, they are expected to produce downward biased forecasts and issue pessimistic forecasts to create future positive earnings surprises.

This research tries to highlight the factor relating to the companies' growth status that influences the management's decision to report pessimistic forecast to produce positive FEs when companies' shares are recommended to sell, and generate optimistic forecast when the companies' shares are recommended to buy. More specifically, this research tries to determine the ability of analysts' recommendations (in terms of buy or sell recommendations) in explaining the reason behind FM.

The next chapter will explain background of regulations about managers' forecasts in the United States.

Chapter 3. BACKGROUND OF REGULATIONS ABOUT MANAGERS' FORECASTS IN THE UNITED STATES

3.1 Introduction

This chapter explains the background of managers' forecast in the United States. I explain the chronological development of the regulations related to managers' forecasts in the United States.

3.2 Background of Managers' Forecasts in the United States

Policy-makers and regulators have long been concerned with the reliability of managers' forecasts. In the United States, the Securities and Exchange Commission (SEC) historically prohibited the inclusion of forward-looking statements in SEC filings because it argued that the market forces were insufficient to induce managers to provide accurate forecasts (Penman 1980; Pownall and Waymire 1989). However, at some points in time, there were some regulations that were in favour of encouraging the management to issue frequent forecasts.

The Private Securities Litigation Reform (PSLR) Act (1995) provides a statutory safe-harbour to shelter managers from litigation arising from the situation where the reported Earnings per Share (EPS) fail to meet the managers' forecast of EPS and hence produce negative *forecast error*. In order to subject the manager to penalties under the antifraud conditions of Section 10(b) of the Securities Exchange Act of 1934 and the SEC proclaimed Rule 10b-54, a plaintiff must be able to establish that a manager's forecast was made with the actual knowledge that it was actually false or misleading, that is, the management has been willingly doing *forecasts management*. It is more onerous for plaintiffs to successfully litigate when it is more difficult to detect misrepresentation (Castura, Litzenberger, Gorelick, & Dwivedi, 2010).

Although Penman (1980); Pownall and Waymire (1989) discuss that firms typically viewed the safe-harbour provision that sheltered them from litigation arising from unattained forward-looking statements in SEC filings as being inadequate, Johnson et al. (2001) found that from the point of view of the managers, it lowered the expected litigation costs associated with unattained forecasts. As Kim & Shi (2010) highlighted, the PSLR Act of 1995 created a safe harbour for forward-looking information. This law protects firms from litigation arising from unattained projections. In passing this law, the regulators were attempting to encourage the release of prospective information in what they believe to be

Informative disclosures that will eventually help investors interpret a company's economic prospects, and are believed to reduce the cost of capital.

Following the enactment of the PSLR Act of 1995 which lowered the expected litigation costs associated with unattained forecasts when accompanied by appropriate cautionary language (Rogers & Stocken, 2005), investors, policy-makers, and regulators were concerned about the reliability of this forward-looking information (e.g., Grundfest and Perino 1997; Johnson, Kasznik, and Nelson 2001). As a result of these concerns, SEC's Regulation Fair Disclosure (Reg. FD) was passed on October 23, 2000.

3.2.1   Regulation Fair Disclosure (Reg FD)

This section first explains the background of regulation fair disclosure and then explains the effect of regulation fair disclosure on the forecasts.

3.2.1.1   *Background*

Before the 1990s, most individual investors followed the progress of their stock holdings by receiving phone calls from their broker, by reading annual or quarterly reports mailed to them by the company, by reading news in newspapers or financial publications, or by calling the company with questions. Most investors relied primarily upon full service brokers, such as Merrill Lynch, for trading advice.

During the 1990s, Internet usage became widespread and online discount brokers allowed individual investors to trade stocks online at the push of a button. At the same time, these investors began using the Internet to research stocks and make timely, more informed trading decisions. By 1999, individual investors became more aware of quarterly analyst conference calls, where a company's management would disclose the results of the quarter and answer analyst questions about the company's past performance and future prospects. At the time, most companies did not allow small investors to attend their calls.

In December 1999, the SEC proposed Regulation FD. Although large institutional investors fought vigorously against the proposed regulation as they argued that fair disclosure would lead to less disclosure, many individual investors wrote the SEC to support for the regulation. In October 2000, the SEC ratified Regulation FD.

Reg FD was promulgated to address the issue of selective disclosure, i.e., firms disclosing material information to a few select investors and analysts. Through selective disclosure, some investors receive material information before other investors and thus benefit from such information. The select few analysts who receive the information in turn "reward" the firm with favourable forecasts and recommendations. Reg FD prohibits such disclosures. It mandates that all publicly traded firms disclose material non-public information to all the investors at the same time. If a firm releases material information to select groups, it must immediately disclose the same information publicly. Firms can choose different venues, such as online webcast, press release, and filing 8-K with the SEC, to disclose material information publicly.

3.2.1.2 *The Effect of Reg FD on Forecasts*

By forcing managers to make use of public forecasts rather than restricted communications, FD prohibits firms from private-only disclosure. Before FD, managers could keep away from publicly recanting previous optimistic forecasts by secretly communicating with analysts, who could decrease investor expectations with a new analyst forecast. After FD, managers with optimistic forecasts need either publicly confess their optimism by providing a new managers' forecast or they must negatively surprise investors at the earnings announcement. This implies the importance and considerations that managers' forecasts have obtained after FD. It also reflects the importance of the end of the year managers' forecasts and its improvement in terms of accuracy. The reason is that by adjusting the previous optimistic forecast management tries to make its forecast more accurate or pessimistic. Heflin et al. (2011) posit that by prohibiting the manager from having private communication with analysts, FD increases pessimism in management earnings forecasts. Heflin et al. (2011) show that FD lowered optimism in managers' forecasts but the decreasing optimistic bias is not counterweighed by a rise in pessimistic bias reflecting progresses in forecast accuracy and informativeness. Heflin et al. (2011) conclude that FD improved firms' forecast properties by making the forecasts to be less biased, have greater accuracy, and greater informativeness.

This improvements in managers' forecast accuracy may, in part, add to the growth in the informational efficiency of stock prices (Hutton & Stocken, 2009) and decrease in the cost of equity capital formerly documented. For example, Chen et al. (Chen, Dhaliwal, & Xie, 2010) and Gomes et al. (2007) suggest that FD reduced the cost of equity capital. In contrast, Albring et al. (2010) suggest that FD has moved financing preferences for firms' with high public-disclosure costs toward debt. This indicates that the companies that have high disclosure costs will less frequently issue earnings forecasts and this will lead to higher information asymmetry. Similarly Eleswarapu et al. (2004), Duarte et al. (2008) and Sidhu et al. (2004) investigate the effect of FD on information asymmetry. They find that Reg FD did not deteriorate information environment for most of the firms. In addition they state that Reg FD has reduced the information asymmetry for some of the firms.

Results regarding FD's effect on analysts' forecasts are mixed. Canace et al. (2008) Heflin, Subramanyam, & Zhang (2012), Herrmann, Hope et al. (2008), Kross and Suk (2010) investigate the impact of FD on expectations management, which is gauged by means of analyst forecasts and actual earnings. They provide evidence that suggests FD decreased expectations management to meet or beat expectations for both U.S. and ADR[1] companies.[0] Bushee et al. (2008) study conference calls (not management earnings forecasts per se) and suggest that pre-FD closed-call firms were more tending to stop or adjust the timing of their calls following FD. Likewise, they show larger conference-call price instability following FD for pre-FD closed-call firms. This indicates that after Reg FD, companies have higher ability to manage the analysts' expectations.

To summarize, based on Reg. FD (2000), no material information should selectively be disclosed. Before the Reg. FD, managers were able to selectively answer questions from analysts and consequently, adjust the decline in stock prices that might result from the issuance of any unfavourable forecasts. In addition,

---

[1] American depositary receipt is a negotiable certificate issued by a U.S. bank representing a specified number of shares in a foreign stock that is traded on a U.S. exchange. This is a method through which U.S. investors can buy shares in a foreign company while realizing any dividends and capital gains in U.S. dollars.

managers were also free to provide earnings guidance as a voluntary disclosure to their selected analyst. Prior researches detailed that countless managers utilized this backchannel extensively (Ajinkya and Gift 1984; Hutton 2005). However, after Reg. FD, such private communication is explicitly prohibited, compelling managers to respond to questions from all analysts regarding unfavourable forecasts in a public setting. Early evidence on Regulation Fair Disclosure suggests that it greatly affects voluntary disclosure practices (Heflin et al., 2012; Hutton & Stocken, 2009).

Anilowski et al. (2007) and Rogers and Bushrik (2008) discovered that the likelihood of issuing a bundled forecast increased after the enactment of Reg. FD. Rogers and Bushrik (2008) also argued that since after the Reg. FD, the management are prohibited from selectively answering questions regarding forecasts, and the only choice that remains for managers is to answer questions publicly through conference calls that are associated with earnings announcements. These avenues provide an opportunity for managers to issue and discuss forecasts, prompting an increase in bundled forecasts after the enactment of Reg. FD.

However, although Reg. FD has not arrested the amount of forward-looking information provided by firms, Baily et al. (2003) and Irani and Karamanou (2003) found that it has apparently decreased the quality of such information (Bushee, Matsumoto, & Miller, 2004; Kross & Suk, 2012).

Two years after the enactment of Reg. FD and as a direct consequence of Enron and WorldCom's scandals, Sarbanes Oxley (SOX) was ratified in 2002. Gong et al. (2003) stated that one of the significant effects of Sarbanes Oxley (2002) (SOX) was to limit the earning management of US companies. Bartov and Cohen (2003) concluded that as a result of SOX (2002) regulation, the intention to meet or beat the analysts' expectations decreased post SOX period. However, Rogers and Stocken (2005) mentioned that the threat of litigation is less likely to deter managers from optimistic forecasting, because it is more difficult to successfully sue them for issuing misleading forecasts than issuing misleading financial statements. The next section extensively details the inconsistency in the research results with regards to the reliability of managers' forecasting in literature. The next section explains the other important regulation in the U.S. history which is Sarbanes Oxley Act.

3.2.2 Sarbanes Oxley Act

The Sarbanes Oxley Act was enacted as a reaction to a number of major corporate and accounting scandals including those affecting Enron, Tyco International, Adelphia, Peregrine Systems and WorldCom. These scandals shook public confidence in the U.S. securities markets.

The Sarbanes-Oxley Act (SOX) became law on 30 July 2002. It was enacted as emergency legislation amid high-profile corporate scandals and is so important that then Securities and Exchange Commission (SEC) chairman William Donaldson (2009) before Congress said, "the Act represents the most important securities legislation since the original federal securities laws of the 1930s." Contemporaneously, the NYSE and NASDAQ adopted new listing standards.

The Sarbanes Oxley Act of 2002 (SOX) is considered one of the most important corporate disclosure and governance reforms in US history. As stated in the preamble of the Act, a primary objective of SOX is "to protect investors by improving the accuracy and reliability of corporate disclosures". The Act covers issues such as auditor independence, corporate, internal control assessment, and enhanced financial disclosure. The SOX requires internal controls for assuring the accuracy of financial reports and disclosures, and mandates both audits and reports on those controls.

The SOX created Public Company Accounting Oversight Board (PCAOB). PCAOB is authorized to establish a registration process for public accountants, create audit standards, engage in inspections of public accountants, and conduct disciplinary hearings. SOX also prohibited an accounting firm from providing audit work for a public company while contemporaneously providing a host of other services. SOX required each public firm to have an audit committee composed of independent directors, and prohibited company loans to certain executives and directors. It also required attorneys for public corporations to report material violations of law to the corporation's chief legal or to the CEO.

A premise underlying Sarbanes-Oxley Act (2002) is that improving corporate governance structures within firms will compel managers to act in the shareholders' best interests. As these regulations impose compliance costs, the results of empirical research into the efficacy of some of the regulatory recommendations are likely to be of interest to regulators and other stakeholders (Bartov & Cohen, 2008).

Several Surveys have been conducted to find whether the positive effect of SOX on investor confidence, reliability of financial statements, and fraud prevention outweigh its costs. For example Arping and Sautner (1978) investigated whether SOX enhanced corporate transparency. Looking at foreign firms that are cross-listed in the US, they indicated that, relative to a control sample of comparable firms that are not subject to SOX, cross-listed firms became significantly more transparent following SOX. Rittenberg and Miller (2005) indicated that in the post SOX period financial statements are perceived to be more reliable compared to the pre SOX period.

Although the SOX has improved the reliability of financial statements, there have been some controversies regarding the relation between the reliability of financial statements and the development of financial markets. Anecdotal evidence (Chan, Faff, Mather, & Ramsay, 2012) and empirical studies (Kasznik, 1999b) suggest that SOX is a significant contributor to restoring investor confidence. However, The Committee on Capital Markets Regulation raises concerns about the effects of SOX on the global competitiveness of U.S. capital markets and calls for the relaxation of some of its rules (Chan et al., 2012).

To test the effect of SOX on the global competitiveness of U.S. capital markets, Jain et al. (2005) considered the market liquidity as an index showing competitiveness of US equity. They investigated the possible effects of financial scandals, Congressional responses (SOX legislation), and related Securities and Exchange Commission (SEC) regulations (SOX implementation rules) on market liquidity. They found that regulatory responses including the Sarbanes-Oxley Act of 2002 (SOX) had inconsequential short-term liquidity effects but highly significant and positive long-term liquidity effects. These liquidity improvements are positively associated with the improved quality of financial reports, and firm-specific variables such as size of the company (Donaldson, 2005).

Regarding the size, previous researches document that SOX affected differently on small and large firms. About the effect of SOX on small firms, Kamar, Karaca-Mandic et al. ("Committee on Capital Markets Regulation, Interim report of the Committee on Capital Markets Regulation," 2006) found that SOX induced small firms to exit the public capital market during the year following its enactment. However, although SOX appears to have had little effect on the going-private propensities of larger firms, Linck et al. (2008) states that, there have been both broad-based changes and officials changes in large firms. Board committees meet more often post-SOX and Director and Officer (D&O) insurance premiums have doubled. Directors post-SOX are more likely to be lawyers/consultants, financial experts, and retired executives, and less likely to be current executives. Post-SOX boards are larger and more independent.

Finally, they find significant increases in director pay and overall director costs, particularly among smaller firms (Jain et al., 2008). Linck et al. (2008) confirms that as a result of SOX firms need to pay people more for the position of a director. They also document that the composition of the boards also changes with relatively more lawyers and financial experts and relatively fewer executives from other firms.

Investors lobbied overwhelmingly in favour of strict implementation of SOX, while corporate insiders and business groups lobbied against strict implementation. Hochberg et al. (2009) found that the companies that are facing agency problems are most affected by the law and are those whose insiders lobbied against strict implementation.

3.2.2.1 *The Effect of SOX on Forecasts*

Regarding the effect of SOX on forecasts, consistent with the view of opportunistic forecasts, Rogers and Stocken (2005) mentioned that the threat of litigation is less likely to deter managers from optimistic forecasting, because it is more difficult to successfully sue them for issuing misleading forecasts than issuing misleading financial statements. However, Gong et al. (2003) stated that one of the significant effects of Sarbanes Oxley (2002) (SOX) was to limit the earning management of US companies. Bartov and Cohen (2009) concluded that as a result of SOX (2002) regulation, the intention to meet or beat the analysts' expectations decreased post SOX period.

However, Stunda (2008) provided empirical evidence, regarding the credibility of managers' forecasts during pre-Sarbanes-Oxley and post Sarbanes-Oxley forecasting periods. His results indicate that managers exerted greater upward earnings management on the forecast during a pre Sarbanes-Oxley environment, but tend to exert greater downward earnings management on the forecast in a post Sarbanes-Oxley environment. In fact, in order to meet forecasts, the management

106

shifted from upward earnings management to downward forecasts management. Stunda's results indicate the presence of incremental information content in managers' forecasts in a post Sarbanes-Oxley environment.

Likewise, Li, Pincus and Rego (2008) showed that investors reacts more positively to firms with aggressive accounting when SOX legislative events occurred because SOX would improve the credibility of these firms' financial reporting. Finally Li, Pincus and Rego (2008) show that, the percentage of change in forecasts revision has decreased in the post-SOX period.

However, Asare (2009) argued that, US analysts presume that the quality of corporate governance in most US companies is relatively low in the absence of independent verification. He believes that, the Sarbanes-Oxley Act (SOX 2002) has not changed corporate governance quality in US companies.

3.3   Summary

By increasing popularity of internet usage in 1990s, individual investors became more aware of quarterly analyst conference calls. In 1995 to encourage the companies to issue forecasts SEC passed the PSLR Act. This Act lowered the expected litigation costs associated with unattained forecasts when accompanied by appropriate cautionary language. However after passage of this Act, investors, policy-makers, and regulators were concerned about the reliability of this forward-looking information.

As a result of such concerns, the FD was passed in 2000. However, although Reg. FD has not arrested the amount of forward-looking information provided by firms, has apparently decreased the quality of such information content in the managers' forecasts.

In addition, in 2002, the SOX put some restrictions on upward earnings management for the companies. Therefore, after SOX it seems that managers have shifted from doing earnings management to forecasts management.

In the next chapter, after developing the hypotheses, the research methods will be explained in detail.

Chapter 4. RESEARCH METHODS

4.1 Introduction

This chapter is devoted to the framework and hypotheses of the study, where detailed explanations regarding the methods that are used to measure the values of the variables are explored. Furthermore, the procedures for empirical testing of the hypotheses are further explained, and the details of the sample are discussed in this chapter. Finally the chapter describes the data's characteristics and

4.2 Research Framework and Hypothesis Development

The framework and hypotheses of this study are based upon a number of assumptions, which are further discussed in the following sections.

4.2.1 Relationship of Optimism/Pessimism with Efficiency and Opportunism

The consensus in the managers' earning forecast literature is that management choose to report forecast due to either voluntary disclosure incentives or for strategic manipulation of the expectations (Cormier & Martinez, 2006).

Voluntary disclosure theory predicts that, the reason that management report forecast is that, the benefits to the firm (and its management) exceed the costs. A maintained assumption of voluntary disclosure models is that the management maximizes shareholder value (i.e., there are no conflicts of interest between the shareholders and the management). This assumption implies that managers' earnings forecasts reported voluntarily (but not opportunistically) are unbiased and they adjust analysts and investors expectations, reduce information asymmetries, reduce litigation risk, etc.

However, the opposing (non-informative) view is that, management issues forecasts to strategically manipulate the stock market expectation. In other words, management issues forecasts to strategically signal good firm performance or to increase stock option compensation.

The next section explains the relationship of managers' forecast informativeness that is emphasized in voluntary disclosure theories, with forecasts optimism. This relationship will help to connect the hypotheses to the existing theories.

4.2.1.1 *Relationship of optimism with informativeness*

According to Dutta and Gigler (2002), since for growth companies issuing high forecasts help them in the process of their financial reporting, thus the high forecasts in the growth companies are considered as informative. The view of Dutta and Gigler is implicitly consistent with several empirical researches.

For example, Clement, Frankel, & Miller (2003) state that, confirming managers' forecasts are voluntary forecasts by management that corroborate existing market expectations about future earnings. They find that the stock market's reaction to confirming forecasts is significantly positive, and such forecasts decrease the cost of capital, showing lesser information asymmetry and thus showing informativeness of such forecasts. Since growth (Buy) companies' forecasts are optimistic and confirm the existing market perception about the company's future performance, according to Clement et al. (2003) they are considered as informative.

The next section explains the relationship of less informative view of forecast with the forecast pessimism.

4.2.1.2 *Relationship of Pessimism with less Informativeness*

Skinner (1994) finds that managers' earnings forecasts are more likely to pre-empt bad news earnings surprises, consistent with managers attempting to reduce litigation risk by issuing preemptive forecasts to adjust investor expectations downward and not to inform the outsiders.

Likewise, Rogers and Stocken (2005) find that managers' earnings forecasts issued by distressed (non-growth) firms are less credible, since forecasts for non-growth firms are not associated with negative price changes (Lopez & Rees, 2002; Payne & Robb, 2000).

Similarly, Koch (2002) examined the relation between financial distress, bias in managers' forecasts, and the credibility of voluntary managers' forecasts. His findings show that, in companies that are financially distressed (non-growth companies), the managers' forecasts are biased, and are less credible than companies that are not financially distressed.

The above empirical findings reveal that the forecasts that are issued by non-growth companies are pessimistic and therefore biased.

The next section explains, how the analysts' recommendations which is used to identify the growth and non-growth companies, help to predict the forecasts pessimism.

4.2.2   Analysts' Recommendations and Pessimism

The analysts' recommendations for buying (or selling) a company's stock(s) may significantly outweigh the recommendations for selling (or buying) the same stocks. This classifies the companies' stocks as either sell or buy, where *buy* companies are assumed to be inherently more profitable than *sell* companies (Ronen & Yaari, 2002). Since the stock prices of buy companies are susceptible to earnings' news, the buy companies can effectively carry out income increasing earnings management (Ronen & Yaari, 2002). Doing so allows buy companies to significantly influence the investors' opinions, which results in effective earnings management. In addition, firms rated as buy are more likely to engage in earnings management that leaves reported earnings equal to, or slightly higher than the analysts' forecasts (Abarbanell & Lehavy, 2003b). However, sell companies are not able to carry out earnings management. This is consistent with the Dutta and Gigler (2002) framework about the growth and non-growth companies.

As explained in chapter 2, assuming that both predicted and reported earnings influence the management's compensation, Dutta and Gigler (2002) develop the following framework.

Dutta and Gigler (2002) assume that the companies are either non-growth and produce low profit (low type company/manager), or the companies are growth and produce high profit (high type company/manager). In the presence of forecasts, Dutta and Gigler (2002) propose optimal communication contracts, in which the non-growth companies who report low forecasts are shielded from the risk associated with the accounting earnings. On the other hand, the optimal contract penalizes the growth companies who reports high forecast when such a report is followed by low accounting income. This penalty must be sufficiently large to ensure that the low type manager does not mimic the high type, by issuing a high forecast and subsequently manipulating earnings. On the other hand, this penalty cannot be too large; otherwise the high type manager will not have incentives to engage in earnings manipulation.

4.2.3 Theoretical Model

Based on the different forecasts management expectations for growth (buy) and non-growth (sell) companies, this study examines the effect of companies' growth capability in terms of analysts' recommendations (AR) on the management's incentive to conduct forecasts management to produce positive forecasts errors. Therefore, the theoretical model of this study is shown in Figure 4-1.

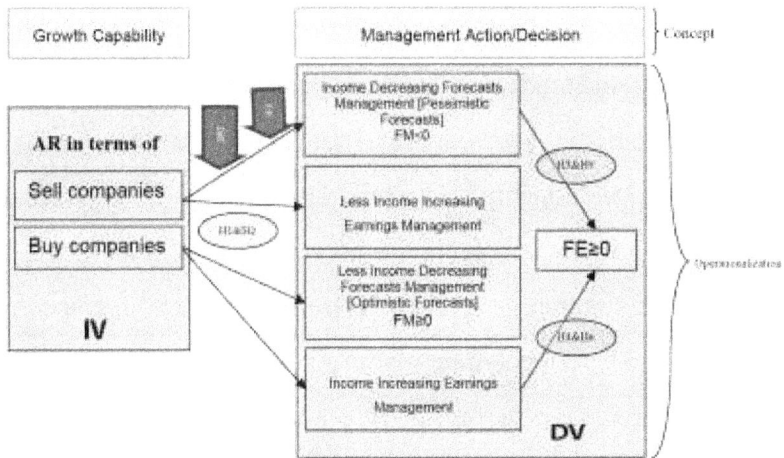

Notes:

Buy companies are the companies that analysts recommend to buy
Sell companies are the companies that analysts recommend to sell
AR = Analysts Recommendations
Diff = Difficulty (Control Variable)
LE = Learning Effect (Control Variable)
FE= Forecast Error
IV= Independent Variable
DV= Dependent Variable
Figure 4-1. Theoretical model of the study.

Consistent with the Dutta and Gigler (2002) framework, and the Figure 4-1the next two sections explain the strategies that buy and sell companies follow to avoid negative earnings surprises.

4.2.4 Analysts' Recommendations and Forecast Management (H1)

In this section, the first hypothesis regarding the relationships between the independent variable (AR) and dependent variable (FM) is developed. The second hypothesis is also developed in respect of the relationship between independent variable (AR) and second dependent variable (FE). Moreover, the hypotheses are drawn up to examine the effect of companies' growth perspective in terms of analysts' recommendation on management incentive to do FM and produce positive FE. Hypotheses 3 and 5 are about the effect of FM on FE in sell companies. Hypotheses 4 and 6 are about the effect of FM on FE in buy companies. Table 4-1 explains the difference in the behaviour of the buy and sell companies.

Table 4-1. Comparison of the reporting processes of the buy and sell companies

Analysts' Recommendation (AR)	Buy (Growth) companies (Abarbanell and Lehavy 2003b)	Sell (non-growth) companies (Abarbanell and Lehavy 2003b)
Incentive	• Have incentive to avoid negative forecasts errors (to prevent fall of stock price) (Abarbanell and Lehavy, 2003b; Dutta and Gigler, 2002)	• Have incentive to avoid negative forecasts errors (to prevent litigation, takeover, contract termination) (Benihrz, 2007; Frost, 1997; Kim & Shi, 2011)
Profitability	• Profitable (Abarbanell and Lehavy, 2003b) • Stock price more susceptible to earnings news (Abarbanell and Lehavy 2003b) • Have significant resources to manipulate earnings (Abarbanell and Lehavy, 2003b)	• Less profitable (Abarbanell and Lehavy 2003b) • Stock price is not susceptible to earnings news (Abarbanell and Lehavy 2003b) • Don't have sufficient resources to manipulate earnings (Abarbanel and Lehavy, 2003b)
Capability to Manipulate Profit	• Can Effectively carry out income increasing earnings management (Abarbanell and Lehavy 2003b, Dutta and Gigler 2002)	• Cannot Effectively manipulate the profit to increase the stock price • Earnings management is potentially costly for them (Abarbanell and Lehavy 2003b, Dutta and Gigler 2002) • Engage in downward forecasts management instead
Forecasts Management (FM)	• Issue Informative/optimistic forecasts (Clement et al. 2003, Dutta and Gigler 2002)	• Manipulate the forecasts Downward • (issue pessimistic/ less informative forecasts) (Rogers and Stocken 2005, Kock 2002, Brown et al. 2005)
Forecasts Errors (FE)	• Meet forecasts	• Report earnings which is equal or higher than forecasts (create positive forecasts errors)

4.2.4.1 *Buy companies*

Abarbanell and Lehavy (2003b) state that, since managers of buy companies possess sufficient resources to effectively manage earnings they can effectively manipulate the profit. In addition, since the buy companies' stock prices are highly susceptible to earnings' news (Abarbanell & Lehavy, 2003b), by reporting optimistic forecast, the management can positively affect the investors' opinion. Therefore, the management of buy companies can effectively carry out income increasing earnings management at low states to report high profit and affect the investors' opinions. Similarly, Dutta and Gigler (2002) state that after issuing high forecasts, management of buy companies conduct income increasing earnings management to meet the forecasts.

On the other hand, the sell companies follow a different strategy to avoid negative FEs. The following section explains the strategies that sell companies follow.

4.2.4.2 *Sell companies*

Sell companies are considered as low profit companies, rendering them unable to effectively conduct income increasing earnings management (Abarbanell & Lehavy, 2003b; Skinner, 1994). This assumption is due to the following reasons, firstly, since sell companies are less vigilantly monitored by investors, their prices are less susceptible to earnings news, making their earnings management ineffective in influencing investors' opinions (Abarbanell & Lehavy, 2003b). In other words, sell companies cannot effectively manipulate and increase low profit to increase stock prices. Secondly; sell companies are companies that have a meagre sum of available accounting reserves or pre-managed earnings to realize any relevant earnings' target (Abarbanell & Lehavy, 2003b). This implies that sell companies do not have the sufficient resources to effectively manage earnings.

Taking into account the aforementioned issues, it seems that unlike the buy companies, if the sell companies issue high forecasts, they are unable to conduct effective earnings management to realize the forecasts afterwards. This makes it more likely for them to miss the forecasts. In order to prevent this from happening, sell companies prefer to issue low forecasts.

For sell companies, if the economic profit is high (which rarely is the case), and high forecasts are issued, the management can quite simply conduct income increasing earnings management after the fact to reach the forecasts, as compared to the time when profits are low. But if profits are low, which often it is, while the management forecast high profits, due to inadequate resources, they are abstained from carrying out income increasing earnings management to reach the forecasted profit. Since for sell companies, the susceptibility of stock price to earnings' news is low, the management will not be goaded into issuing high forecasts reflecting positive news. In addition, their inability to effectively manage earnings prevents management of sell companies from issuing high forecasts. The failure of sell companies, in realizing forecasts exposes the management to several risks, namely, litigation risk, contract termination risk and takeover risk (Beniluz, 2007; Frost, 1997; Kim & Shi, 2011). Therefore, consistent with Dutta and Gigler's (2002) proposition, it is optimal to make earnings management potentially costly for management of sell companies.

Therefore, if the company is in the sell position, the management may issue lower forecasts in order to dampen the expectation of outsiders (Li, Wasley, & Zimmerman, 2010). Since such pessimistic forecast does not convey the management's true expectation to the market, it is considered as an opportunistic action, according to literature. Based on the result of the firm's ordinary operation, the management would then report an earning which is equal to or higher than the forecast (report positive forecast error), as doing so will raise the bids for the company's stocks, and subsequently, increase the company's stock price.

This prediction for sell companies is consistent with several empirical findings. For example, Stunda (2003) found that that the management of companies that meet the forecasts are more likely to issue estimations that they could actually reach. Additionally, Ivković & Jegadeesh (2003) found that the content of information and the resultant negative price effect of downward forecast revision near earnings announcement is insignificant. Therefore, the first hypothesis would be:

H1: Sell companies issue more pessimistic forecasts than buy companies.

4.2.5 Analysts' Recommendations and Frequency of Forecast Errors (H2)

Prior researches have confirmed that since negative FE could cause a negative shock in the stock market and deteriorate management (company) status, the management engage in FM to avoid negative FEs (Choi et al., 2006; Stunda, 2008; Sun & Xu, 2012). This is done because the management perceives the negative price effect of producing downward biased forecast is less than the future positive price effect of positive FE (Cormier & Martinez, 2006; Payne & Robb, 2000).

Buy companies are growth companies and enjoy high profit. Missing the forecasts in the buy companies lead to decrease in the stock price. However, sell companies suffer from an unsatisfactory stock market, the management's motivation to conduct downward forecast management is expected to be higher. This is due to the fact that sell companies usually suffer from poor earnings performance, which would be a glaring evidence of managerial incompetence (Abarbanell & Lehavy, 2003b). Missing the forecasts for sell companies would cost managers the support of stockholders and potentially their very own jobs (Bowen et al., 1995; Shan, Taylor, & Walter, 2012).

Since failure in realizing forecasts exposes the sell companies to severe risks, namely, litigation risk, contract termination risk and takeover risk (Beniluz 2007, Frost 1997, Kim

& Shi 2011), sell companies are more expected to meet their forecasts and avoid the negative FEs. Thus, it is expected that sell companies have higher frequency of positive FEs (earnings surprises) than buy companies, therefore, the second hypothesis would be:

H2: Sell companies have higher frequency of positive forecasts errors than buy companies.

The Figure 4-2 simplifies the operationalization of the H2.

Figure 4-2. Operationalization of the second hypothesis.
In the sell companies, management often decreases the forecast
to produce positive forecast error.

4.2.6 Forecasts Management and Positive Forecasts Errors (H3 and H4)

Brown and Caylor (2002) state that investors unambiguously reward firms for reporting earnings that meet their forecasts and penalize firms for reporting earnings that miss their forecasts. This is because investors use heuristics cut-offs, such as earnings forecast, to determine the terms of transactions with a firm. The use of heuristics often arises as a response to the information's costs in economic models (Conlisk, 1996). When it is costly for stakeholders to retrieve and process detailed information on earnings for all firms with which they deal with (explicitly and implicitly), it is assumed that certain stakeholders use heuristic cut-offs such as zero or positive forecasts errors. According to Bird et al. (2000), Ivković and Jegadeesh (2004), Choi, Myers et al. (2006) and King et al. (1990), such heuristic cut-off could be managers' forecast error.

Consistent with this, the prospect theory postulates that decision-makers make decisions based on the potential value of losses and gains rather than the final outcome, and such gains and losses are based on reference points, like managers' forecasts (Choi et al., 2006; Ivković & Jegadeesh, 2004; King et al., 1990), rather than from the company's real outcome. It is also suggested that the value function is defined on deviations from a reference point and is normally concave for gains (implying risk aversion), commonly convex for losses (risk seeking) (S-shaped) and is generally steeper for losses than for gains (loss aversion) (Arya et al., 1998). In other words, the value functions are steepest around wealth reference points. Thus, for a given increase in wealth, the corresponding increase in value is greatest when the increase in wealth shifts the individual from a loss to a gain relative to a reference point.

This provides enough incentives for sell companies to decrease their forecasts in order to create future positive forecasts errors, because taking into account the S-shaped value function in Burgstahler and Dichev (1998), they can invariably avoid the market punishment.

The companies that analysts recommend to sell (sell companies) are the companies that does not have high growth capabilities and suffer from poor performance, which would be a glaring evidence of managerial incompetence (Abarbanell & Lehavy, 2003b). These companies are already affected by the unsatisfactory condition of the stock market. If they miss forecasts, they risk further deterioration of the market state. However, unlike the buy companies, the sell companies do not possess enough resources and have less accounting flexibility to manipulate the profit and meet their forecasts. Hence, sell companies seek to find an alternative method to meet the forecasts.

Therefore, if the company is in the sell position, the management may issue lower forecast in order to dampen the expectation of outsiders (Li et al., 2010). Based on the result of the firm's ordinary operation, the management would then report an earning which is equal to or higher than the forecast (report positive forecast error), as doing so will raise the bids for the company's stocks, and subsequently, increase the company's stock price.

Thus, if FM in sell companies is effectively conducted to achieve positive FE, then companies that meet the forecasts should have conducted higher income decreasing FMs than the companies that miss the forecasts. Following this logic, the following hypotheses should be supported in the context of sell companies.

H3: In sell companies, those that meet forecasts are more likely to do income decreasing FM than those that do not meet forecasts.

For buy companies, it is important to meet the forecasts and negative forecasts errors cause negative shock in the stock price. Buy companies have high profitability and therefore have enough resources to manipulate the earnings (Abarbanell & Lehavy, 2003b; Dutta & Gigler, 2002). Therefore, buy companies can efficiently manage the earnings to meet their forecasts. Thus, in the buy companies, companies that meet forecasts do not necessarily do income decreasing FM to meet forecasts[1] . Thus, the[1]present study expects the fourth hypothesis for the buy companies to be supported.

H4: There is no significant difference in income decreasing FM between buy companies that meet forecasts and those that do not meet forecasts.

4.2.7 Analysts' Recommendations, Positive Forecast Errors and "Unmanaged" vs. Issued Forecast (H5 and H6)

In order to develop a more robust test for FM among the companies that meet or do not meet forecasts; H5 and H6 were formulated.

The reason more robust tests are required is the fact that it is possible, despite the companies meeting forecasts produce downward biased forecasts, the income decreasing FM might not aim for positive FE; instead, it might be due to other reasons such as corralling the analysts' expectations downward (Baginski & Hassell, 1990).

---

1 However, Accoِrding to Abarbanell and Lehavy (2003b), and Dutta and Gigler (2002) the buy (growth) companies are likely to do income increasing earnings management to meet forecasts and produce positive earnings surprises.

FE is calculated as the difference between forecasted EPS and reported EPS. Similarly, pre-managed/unbiased forecast can be used instead of forecasted EPS to calculate FE (Chin, Kleinman, Lee, & Lin, 2006).

If forecasts management in sell companies is only conducted to realize positive FEs, then the frequency of positive FEs that are calculated by "unmanaged" forecasts should be significantly lower than the frequency of positive FEs that are calculated by "managed" (issued) forecasts. Following this, the fifth hypothesis is accurate for sell companies.

H5: For sell companies, the frequency of positive forecasts errors is expected to decrease when forecasts errors are based on "unmanaged" rather than issued forecasts.

The income decreasing FM by the sell companies are conducted to achieve positive FEs, whereas buy companies forecasts are optimistic and they supposedly do not have income decreasing FM. Thus, in buy companies, the frequency of positive FEs that is calculated by "unmanaged" forecasts should not be different from frequency of positive FEs that is calculated by "managed" (issued) forecasts. Therefore, contradicting my prediction for sell companies, the prediction of forecasts management and forecasts errors should not hold for buy companies. The sixth hypothesis is formulated to test the FEs and

FM for buy companies. The sixth hypothesis is accurate for buy companies.

H6: The frequency of positive forecasts errors for buy companies is not expected to decrease when forecasts errors are based on "unmanaged" rather than issued forecasts.

The next section describes the procedure employed to test the hypotheses.

4.3   Methods

Research is a complex process and complicated by a variety of expectations. Given this complexity, it may not be surprising that scholars build their endeavours on differing beliefs about how research should be done and what the results of the study should achieve (Krauss, 2005). These differing beliefs are categorized under three paradigms, namely, positivist, interpretivist and critical research (Krauss, 2005). Accordingly, the methodology employed should match the particular paradigm (Krauss, 2005). Generally, there are three dominant paradigms in accounting research, the positivist, interpretivist and critical (Chua, 1986). In this study, the positivist paradigm is most appropriate to reflect the research objectives as explained below.

In the positivist paradigm, the object of research is independent of researches including facts are determined by taking apart a phenomenon to examine its component parts and knowledge is found out and verified via direct measurements of phenomena (Healy & Perry, 2000; Krauss, 2005). Positivist researcher usually utilizes quantitative data (Darke, Shanks, & Broadbent, 1998; Krauss, 2005; Landry & Banville, 1992). In addition, in positivist paradigm, researchers develop hypotheses, and then try to disprove these assumed relationships by concentrating on the null hypotheses (Krauss, 2005). In positivist paradigm, data is collected using quantitative data and analysed using statistical methods (Krauss, 2005). In positivist paradigm, another researcher should be able to conduct the same study in the same way and achieve with comparable results (Darke et al., 1998). Therefore, according to the above discussion, this study uses deductive reasoning – beginning with the theoretical framework and moving towards real empirical evidence using the quantitative method – to identify a set of universal laws that can be used to predict general systems of human activity (Krauss, 2005; Landry & Banville, 1992).

In general, this study explains laws that can be predicted by using quantitative methods, hence this is consistent with the positivist paradigm, whereas an interpretivist paradigm focuses on the context and singular occurrences to obtain meaning and making sense, naturally utilizing quantitative approaches (Krauss, 2005;

Lincoln & Guba, 2000; Trauth & Jessup, 2000). Therefore, it is not appropriate to meet the objectives of this study.

Therefore, this study used the empirical method to obtain a large sample so that results can be generalizable to a larger context. The main objective of this section is to explain the process of how data is collected, how the sample is determined, how the variables are measured and how the data is analysed in order to test the hypotheses developed to meet the research objectives. This research used the secondary data.

4.3.1 Independent, Dependent, Moderating and Control Variables

In general, research is a procedural process of getting information with the purpose of findings a solution to specific problems. In the empirical study, the variables should examine the properties, and are employed to test the hypotheses that are identified at the first stage of the study (Cooper, Schindler, & Sun, 2003). There are four types of variables such as independent, dependent, and control variables, investigated in this study. The independent variable is the analysts' recommendations, while the dependent variables are the managers' forecasts management and the managers' forecasts errors. Hence, all the measurement items were generated from prior studies. The measurements of the variables are discussed in the next sections.

4.3.1.1 *Independent Variable Analysts' Recommendations*

Following Heidle and Li (1998) and Abarbanell and Lehavy (2003b), it is believed that the perception of the companies' future growth is reflected in the analysts' recommendations. Analysts' recommendations fluctuate less than bid and ask spread (Frankel et al., 1995), and ask and bid prices (Darke et al., 1998). So they are less affected by market sentiments and they are more reliable in capturing the company's growth perspective.

Analysts' recommendations come in five forms, namely (i) strong buy, (ii) buy, (iii) hold, (iv) sell and (v) strong sell. The rating assigned to each recommendation is displayed in Table 4-2.

Table 4-2. Recommendations and their assigned ratings

Recommendations	Strong buy	buy	hold	sell	Strong sell
Rating	1	2	3	4	5

Following Abarbanell and Lehavy (Abarbanell & Lehavy, 2003b), this research uses the outstanding average (consensus) recommendations at the end of each day in the first, middle, and last three weeks of the first month of the fourth quarter. The average recommendation for firm i, on date t is assumed to be A_{it}.

Each observation is placed in one of three portfolios. The first portfolio consists of firms for which $A_{it} \leq 2$ (denoted "Buy" stocks), the second portfolio includes firms for which $2 < A_{it} \leq 3$ ("Hold" stocks), and the third contains the least favourably recommended firms, for which $A_{it} > 3$ ("Sell" stocks).

The number of buy and sell company years and the criteria for dividing them is shown in the Table 4-3.

Table 4-3. The number of buy, hold and sell company years which is calculated on the basis of consensus analysts' recommendations

	BUY	HOLD	SELL
Consensus analysts' recommendations = A_{it}	$A_{it} \leq 2$	$2 < A_{it} \leq 3$	$3 < A_{it}$
No of companies in each category	817	1204	2468

In order to compare means (ANOVA tables) in section 5.3.3.1.2 (on page193) and for the contingency table in section5.2.3.1.1 (on page 191), since the extreme growth (buy) and non-growth (sell) companies are taken into account, the hold companies are omitted.

The next sections explain the methods for measuring the dependent variables.

4.3.1.2 *Dependent Variables Forecast Management*

Forecast Management is measured using several procedures. The procedures are clarified as follows.

The management may issue forecast at the start of a new fiscal year. During the year, as a result of obtaining new information, the management may increase, decrease or remain unchanged in their initial forecasts. This increase or decrease in the managements' forecasts is dubbed the forecast revision (Matsumoto 2002, Burgestahler and Eams 2005). The following computation is used for the determination of Forecast Revision (FR):

$$FR = \frac{Last\ Mgmt.\ Forecast\ of\ EPS - First\ Mgmt.\ Forecast\ of\ EPS}{Share\ Price\ of\ the\ Company\ at\ the\ End\ of\ Fourth\ Quarter} \qquad (4\text{-}1)$$

Following Wang (2003), Matsumoto (2002) and Burgestahler and Eams (2005), forecasts revision is the first measure that is taken as an indicator of forecasts management. Wang (2003), Matsumoto (2002) and Burgestahler and Eams (2005) argue that forecasts issued early in the fiscal year can be considered as forecasts that exclude forecasts management during the latter part of the year. Therefore, they consider the difference between the late and early annual forecasts as a proxy for forecasts management occurring between the early and late forecast periods. The first proxy for forecast management, which is the difference in the last and first forecast horizons, captures the forecast management occurring between the designated periods.

As Wang (2003), Matsumoto (2002) stated, forecast revision is not an absolute measure of forecasts management, as forecasts revision could also result from new information, as well as forecast management.

Thus, Forecast Revision (FR) comprises of two components, namely New Information $(NEWINF)$, and Forecast Management (FM). To measure FM, the effect of $NEWINF$ must be excluded from FR. The mathematical modelling of this argument is as follows:

$$FR_i = NEWINF_i + FM_i \qquad\qquad (4-2)$$

Where,

i represents the company.

By regressing FR on $NEWINF$, the estimated residual can be assumed to be Forecast Management (Wang, 2003). In other words, supposing that there is a reliable measure for $NEWINF$, the following regression can be used for estimating the value of forecasts management. In order to eliminate the effect of new information $NEWINF$ from FR, equation (4-3) will be estimated in Eviews:

$$FR_i = \alpha NEWINF_i + C + \varepsilon \qquad\qquad (4-3)$$

Where:

C is a constant.

The residuals is generated, and considered as FM.

Considering regression (4-3), although the data for FR is readily available, the issue is the measurement of $NEWINF$. Prior researches have used a number of methods to explain the new information.

This study refers to Wang (2003) to measure the management's forecast revisions. In order to measure the analysts' forecasts management, she uses the change in the reported income from first to third quarter as a proxy for new information. She excludes the information on the fourth quarter's income in order to avoid an endogeneity problem. She also argues that the reason for this is that if it is used, then both *FMINFO* (sum of forecast management in the fourth quarter and the new information) and income changes will be under the effect of unobservable new information in the fourth quarter. This method has its weaknesses which include missing vital information that might be present in the fourth quarter. Furthermore, the method assumes income recognition as annually constant, which blatantly contradicts common occurrences in certain industries.

To overcome the restrictions prior return is used as a proxy for new information. However, Wang (2003) did not use prior return as a measure of new information because she measured the analysts' forecasts management instead of management's forecasts management. The problem with using prior return is that the prior return is a function of both forecast management and new information. This essentially brings about a tautology, or in econometric terminology, an endogeneity problem in the regression (4-3).

However, the focus of this research is in measuring the management's forecasts management, rendering the endogeneity problem negligible. This is due to the fact that managers' forecasts, which are mostly issued with the fourth/final quarter, do not affect the prior new information in the first three quarters that were actually present before the forecast issuance time. Therefore, it is assumed that the return, prior to the time of the fourth quarter forecasts announcement or prior to the time of third quarter's earnings announcement, is a good measure of new information (Matsomoto 2002).

The prior return is measured using the following formula:

$$Return_i = \frac{P_{i,Q3} - P_{i,Q1}}{P_{i,Q1}} \qquad (4-2)$$

Where,

$P_{i,Q3}$ is the stock price at the end of quarter 3 for firm i

$P_{i,Q1}$ is the stock price at the beginning of quarter 1 for firm i

The reason why I do not include the fourth quarter's price in the return formula is that its price would most probably be determined after the issuance of the management's forecast. Hence, the stock price of the fourth quarter could be well affected by the fourth quarter's managers' forecast. This leads to a correlation of new information, and its residual (forecast management), which fails under the preview of endogeneity problem.

In contrast, such problem is non-existent if the price at the end of third quarter is used as an index for new information, since forecasts management is only embedded in the forecast issued in fourth quarter.

One important assumption in using return as an indicator of the management's new information of reported earnings is that the change in price (return), which reflects the new information that the investors in the stock market obtain during the year, is a proxy for new information that the management obtains throughout the year. This assumption is imperative, due to the fact that in efficient markets; the management and investors have similar expectations regarding future earnings.

However, in order to use the most accurate measure of forecasts management, another method, which is an instrumental variable method, developed by Wang (2003), is also utilized. In this method, as shown earlier, FR consists of two parts; forecasts management and new information which are represented by $FMINF$ in the following formula.

$$FMINF_{i,t} = m_{i,t} + n_{i,t} \qquad\qquad (4\text{-}5)$$

Where,

$m_{i,t}$ represents forecasts management of firm i in the period t

$n_{i,t}$ represents new information of firm i in the period t.

Wang (2003) argues that the forecasts management portion of the variable $FMINF$ is firm specific. So, this variable is sensitive to the factors related to the company's characteristics such as litigation costs, shareholder lawsuits and long run reputation of the company. Forecasts management portion of the variable $FMINF$ is persistent throughout the years, in contrast to new information, which varies annually.

Due to the existence of firm specific characteristics regressing $FMINF_{i,t}$ to $FMINF_{i,t-1}$ results in the following:

$$FMINF_{i,t} = \alpha_0 + \alpha_1 FMINF_{i,t-1} + \in_{i,t} \qquad (4\text{-}6)$$

Where, α_1 should not be equal to zero. If α_1 is not equal to zero, then it is confirmed that $FMINF_{i,t}$ has one persistent portion, and that is forecasts management.

In addition, assuming that α_1 is positive $FMINF_{i,t-1}$ satisfies two conditions of a valid instrumental variable. The first condition is that $FMINF_{i,t}$ is highly correlated with $FMINF_{i,t-1}$, meaning $FMINF$ is a positive function of $FMINF_{t-1}$

$FMINF_{i,t-1}$ also satisfies the second condition of being a valid independent variable, by being uncorrelated to n. Assuming that $FMINF_{i,t-1} = m_{i,t-1} + n_{i,t-1}$, and assuming that n is uncorrelated with m, and previous new information is uncorrelated with the current new information, then $Cor(FMINF_{i,t-1}, n_{i,t}) = 0$. These assumptions are well grounded, as the arrival of new information is a purely random event, which means that it is uncorrelated to both across time and forecasts management. In short, Wang (2003) has determined a reliable instrument that correlates with $FMINF$, via forecasts management. The fitted value from the equation above is utilized as another measure of forecasts management, which is dubbed FM_lag.

The other proxy for forecasts management is the one developed by Matsumoto (2002), and later used by Burgstahler and Eames (2002).

Following Burgstahler and Eames (2002) and Matsumoto (2002),another proxy for forecasts management is measured as follows:

$$\frac{\Delta EPS_{ijtq}}{P_{ijtq-4}} = b_{0ij} + b_{1ijt}\left(\frac{\Delta EPS_{ijtq-1}}{P_{ijtq-5}}\right) + b_{2ijt}CRET_{ijtq} + \varepsilon_{ijtq} \quad (4-7)$$

where,

Subscripts refer to firm i, industry code j, quarter q, and year t, and

ΔEPS_{ijtq}= earnings per share changes between the current quarter and four quarters prior.

P_{ijtq}= price per share of common equity, and

$CRET_{ijtq}$= cumulative daily excess returns from three days after the four quarters prior earnings announcement to 20 days before the current quarter earnings announcement.

b_{1ijt} and b_{2ijt}= the coefficients of the regression.

Similar to Matsumoto (2002), first the model for each firm-year is estimated by using all firm quarters of the year from the same industry, except those from firms for which the parameters are estimated. Second, I include only firm-years with 10 or more firm-quarters of data in the same industry in the estimation. Third, observations with variable values in the top and bottom half per cent of the respective distributions are deleted in order to lessen the impact of extreme values on the parameter estimates. Then, the parameter estimates that were obtained were used to determine the expected earnings changes from the prior firm year's fourth quarter:

$$E\left(\Delta EPS_{ijtq}\right) = b_{0ij-1} + b_{1ijt-1}\left(\Delta EPS_{ijtq-1}\right) +$$

$$b_{2ijt-1}(CRET_{ijtq})P_{ijtq-4} \qquad (4\text{-}8)$$

This expected change is added to earnings per share from the same quarter in the prior year in order to obtain the expected forecast $Fijtq$ of the current quarter's earnings:

$$E\left(F_{ijtq}\right) = EPS_{ijtq-4} + E\left(\Delta EPS_{ijtq}\right) \qquad (4\text{-}9)$$

Consequently, to obtain the expected forecast of annual earnings, I estimated the fourth quarter expected earnings (from Equation 4-9), and add the prior three quarters of earnings realizations. Istook into account the differences between the last reported forecast and the model-derived expected forecast as a proxy for forecasts management.

The next section explains how to determine the measure of forecast management that is appropriate for the purpose of testing the hypotheses.

4.3.1.3 *Choosing the Appropriate Measure of Forecasts Management*

Burgstahler and Eames (2006) argue that the benefit of forecast management to a firm should increase the amount of forecast management, however, forecast management also imposes an unduly cost to the firm. If there is a sudden drop in the marginal benefit at the point just to the right of the zero-surprise point for many firms, then zero surprise is the optimal level a firm should achieve by conducting forecast management. In reality, there might indeed be a sudden drop in the marginal benefit for many firms. The benefit to firms of just (barely) meeting expectations is much larger than that for firms that just fail to meet expectations by a small margin, whereas the benefit to firms that beat expectations is only marginally larger than that of firms that just (barely) meet expectations. This argument implies that firms

144

that just (barely) meet expectations are more likely to conduct forecast management than firms that just fail to meet expectations and firms that just beat expectations.

Based on the above arguments, the appropriate measure of forecasts management is examined by plotting the distribution of forecasts management measures against earnings surprises. The plot involves all firms, and consistent with the findings of Burgstahler and Eams (2002), the plots of forecast management measured against earnings surprises, which resulted in a small "V" shape around zero FE. This shows that a significant number of firms manage forecasts downward in order to just (barely) meet expectations. Therefore, it is assumed that an appropriate measure of forecasts management can capture this effect. The next section presents the plot of the distribution of forecasts management against earnings surprise.

4.3.1.4   *The relationship of forecasts management and forecasts Errors*

Figure 4-3 shows four different forecasts management measures against earnings surprises. It can be surmised from the figure that firms manage forecasts downward to meet or beat expectations.

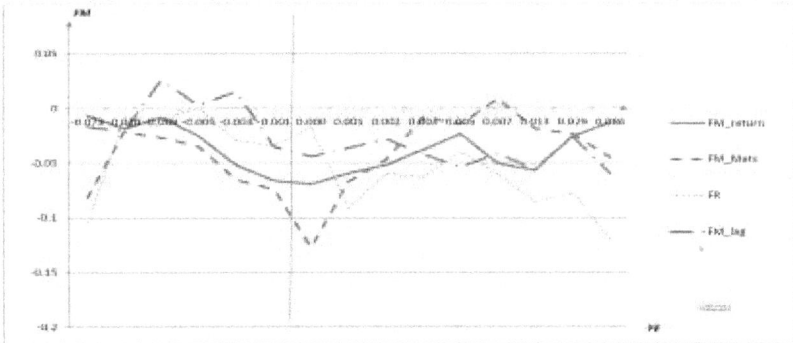

Figure 4-3. Plot of forecasts management models against forecasts errors,
All forecasts management measures are multiplied by 10 for ease of presentation

Figure 4-3 indicates that the plots of FM for *FR* and *FM_lag* are decreasing from negative to positive forecasts errors. In other words, when the larger distance around zero-earning surprise is considered, the value of *FR* and *FM_lag* is substantially lower at the right side of the zero-earnings surprise. Figure

4-3shows that there is constant decrease in the value of the *FM_lag* when the forecasts errors increase.

However, the plots for *FM_Matsumoto* and *FM_return* show only a sharp decrease at zero forecast errors, and are relatively flat on the far left and far right side of zero-earnings surprise. The plot for *FM_Matsumoto* and *FM_return* are consistent with the findings of Burgstahler and Eams (2002); the plots of forecast management against earnings surprises which forms a small "V" shape around zero earnings surprise is evidence of a significant number of firms managing downward forecasts to just meet the expectations. Therefore, it is assumed that an appropriate measure of forecasts management is capable of capturing this effect. As evident in Figure 4-3, the plot of *FM_Matsumoto* and *FM_return* culminated in a "V" shape at zero-earnings surprise. This "V" shape is deeper for *FM_Matsumoto*.

If firms manage downward forecasts just to meet or beat expectations, then firms with zero or small earnings surprises should have relatively large negative forecasts managements. This is evident in Figure 4-3. There is a small "V" shape around zero-earnings surprise point for *FM_return* and *FM_Matsumoto*, and the bottom of the "V" is at zero-earnings surprise. Even though the decrease in forecasts management at the right of zero-earnings surprise (in the form of "V" shape) is very small, such a small "V" shape is consistent with Matsumoto (2002) prediction that firms having zero and small earnings surprises are more likely to manage downward forecasts than firms in the immediate neighbourhood of zero surprise, or firms with slightly larger or smaller earnings surprises.

In Figure 4-3, the value of FM for *FM_Matsumoto* at the right side of zero forecasts error is considerably lower than the value of *FM_Matsumoto* at the left side of the zero forecast error. It is possible that the reason for managing downward forecasts is to reach positive forecasts errors. Based on this assumption, and because the issue of managing downward forecasts to produce positive earnings surprises is consistent with previous findings

(Matsumoto 2002), where the management manage the downward forecasts to produce positive earnings surprises.

In both the *FM_Return* and *FM_Matsumoto* graphs of forecasts management against earnings surprises, it is observed that there is a decrease in the value of forecasts management on the right side of zero earnings surprise. Therefore, by taking into account two measures of forecasts management of *FM_Return* and *FM_Matsumoto*, it is observed that companies do downward forecasts management to reach zero or small positive earnings surprises, which is consistent with previous findings (Matsumoto 2002, Burgestahler & Eams 2005, Kasznik 1999). The plots of *FM_Matsumoto*, measured against earnings surprises (Figure 4-3), provide at least some weak evidence that a significant number of firms manage forecasts in order to just meet expectations.

Therefore, to avoid confusion, the results of the tests with *FM_lag*, *FR* and *FM_Return* are disregarded, and only the results of the tests with *FM_Matsumoto*are reported.

The following section explains the measurement of the next dependent variable which is managers' forecasts errors.

4.3.1.5 *Dependent Variable - Forecasts Errors*

According to Fang (2009), Rogers and Stocken (2011) and Xu (2010),Managers' Forecast Error (FE) is the difference between the company's (management's) predicted (forecasted) and the reported earnings per share. The allocated formula is presented below:

$$MFE = \frac{(Forecasted\ EPS - Reported\ EPS)}{Share\ price\ of\ the\ Company\ at\ the\ End\ of\ 4th\ Quarter} \quad (4\text{-}10)$$

4.3.1.6 *Unbiased forecast error*

Forecast errors (FE) are calculated as the difference between forecasted EPS and reported EPS deflated by the share price of the company at the end of 4th quarter. Similarly, reported EPS and pre-managed/unbiased forecast of EPS can be used to calculate forecast errors. The unbiased forecast is obtained by deducting forecast management from the reported forecast (Felleg, Moers, & Renders, 2012):

Unmanaged forecast
$= (Reported\ forecast - forecast\ management)$ $(4-11)$

I calculate two forecast errors. First, I calculate forecast errors based on deviations between reported forecast of EPS (without any revisions) and actual earnings, and I term it "forecasts errors based on reported forecast" (refer to Section 4.3.1.5).

Second, I calculate forecast error based on unbiased forecasts of EPS and reported EPS, and denote this "forecast error based on unbiased forecast". It signifies the magnitude of forecast errors in the absence of forecasts management.

$$Unmanaged\ FE = \frac{(Unmanafed\ Forecast\ of\ EPS - ReportedEPS)}{Share\ price\ of\ the\ Company\ at\ the\ End\ of\ 4th\ Quarter} \qquad (4\text{-}12)$$

The next section explains the control variables.

4.3.2   Moderating/Control Variables

4.3.2.1   *Measuring Learning Effect (Moderating/Control Variable)*

Previous researches (Ahmed, Billings, & Morton, 2004; Dye, 1988) show that the practice of forecast management is influenced by either positive market responses to meeting or beating market expectations or negative responses associated with a failure to do so.

However, the market can learn from a firm's forecast management behaviour over a period of time. Although the market cannot immediately provide new information from forecast management, it will determine the difference(s) over time. New information can be verified when the market subsequently learns more. If the market can identify new information from history, then it is also capable of identifying forecast management. If the market discerns from a firm's history that it has habitually engaged in downward forecast management, it may expect a behavioural repeat from that particular firm than from firms with a clean history. Consequently, market expectations will be weakly affected by the current forecast management, and the market will react less to an earnings surprise from such firms (Wang 2003, Rogers and Stocken 2005).

Because the market becomes less sensitive to a firm's downward forecast management, and the subsequent positive earnings surprise when a firm manages forecasts downward frequently, a rational firm may find it in its interest not to manage forecasts downward frequently. More specifically, because the cost (benefit) of forecast management increases (declines) with the number of times it has been used in previous periods, the more number of times a firm has biased forecast downward in the past, the less likely it will do so in the current period (Rogers & Stocken, 2005; Wang, 2003).

As Wang (2003) states, the more forecast management a firm conducts in its history, the less likely it will conduct one in the current period. In accordance with Wang (2003), in order to include the learning effect in the relationship of analysts' recommendations and forecasts management, I use a moderating variable, which reflects the frequency of forecasts management (FREQ). Depending on the number of times the firm has had downward FM in four previous periods, this variable can have the value of 1, 2, 3, or 4. The FREQ variable is used and moderating variable in the equation (4-13). However, it will be used as control variable in the equation (4-14).

4.3.2.2 *Measurement of Difficulty (Control Variable)*

Rogers & Stocken (2010) say that managers' incentives to misrepresent their information caused by the threat of litigation is a function of the difficulty market participants experience in detecting manager misrepresentation. Similarly, It is hypothesized that Managers' incentive to misrepresent their information caused by the stock transaction status is a function of the difficulty market participants experience in detecting manager's misrepresentation. Managers' incentive to offer biased forecasts as result of market incentives is attenuated by the market's ability to detect misleading forecasts.

Difficulty reflects the degree of the market participants' ability to assess the credibility of a management's forecasts. The more difficult it is for managers to forecast accurately, the harder it is for the market to assess the credibility of the management's forecasts. According to Rogers and Stocken (2005), there are several variables (indicators) that capture the difficulty of forecasting earnings accurately, and by using these variables, I use factor analysis to identify the difficulty construct. It is assumed that the indicator specific variances are uncorrelated across variables. Consistent with the goal of predicting forecast management, all variables are measured prior to the release of the forecasts.

The following indicator variables generate a measure of forecasting difficulty (Rogers & Stocken, 2005):

- When earnings are difficult to predict, it is expected that analysts to disagree with the forthcoming earnings. The standard deviation of analyst forecasts is outstanding when the managers' forecast is released, and STD_AF measures the lack of analyst consensus.
- If the difficulty the analysts are experiencing in forecasting earnings is correlated with time, then the variability of the previous analyst forecast errors is positively associated with the current difficulty of forecasting earnings. The standard

deviation of the previous analysts' forecasts errors, scaled by price for five years prior to the forecast release, STD_AFE, proxies for the difficulties analysts experienced when predicting earnings.

- It is more difficult to forecast a firm's earnings when the firm is unprofitable compared to when it is profitable. To recognize this asymmetry, the indicator Lagged-Loss equals 1 when a firm's quarterly earnings report preceding the forecast is negative, and 0 if otherwise. Also, the indicator of Predict-Loss equals to 1 when the managers' forecast of earnings is negative, and 0 if vice versa.

- It may be more difficult to forecast a firm's earnings when its "true" earnings are more volatile. "True" earnings are regarded as those that would be reported in the absence of the strategic manipulation or smoothing of earnings. Volatility in the firm's "true" earnings are positively associated with volatility in a firm's stock price, measured as the standard deviation of the daily stock price for 120 days before the forecast date; denoted as *STD_RET*.

- A firm's bid-ask spread is associated with a market specialist's perception of information asymmetry in the market, which is expected to increase with uncertainty regarding the firm's forthcoming earnings announcement (see Coller and Yohn 1997).

The difficulty variable is used and moderating variable in the equation (4-13). However, it will be used as control variable in the equation (4-14). The next section explains the process used for building the variable difficulty.

4.3.2.3 *Factor Analysis for Difficulty*

4.3.2.3.1 **Exploratory Factor Analysis (EFA)**

In multivariate statistics, exploratory factor analysis (EFA) is a statistical technique used to reveal the fundamental formation of a fairly big set of variables. EFA is a method within factor analysis whose main goal is to recognize the fundamental associations among measured variables (Baginski et al., 2011). It is normally used by academics when developing a scale and serves to identify a set of latent constructs underlying a battery of measured variables (Baginski & Hassell, 1990). It should be applied when the researcher has no a priori hypothesis about factors or patterns of measured variables (Emami et al., 2012). *Measured variables* are any one of numerous features that may be seen and gauged. Scientists should vigilantly study the number of measured variables to incorporate in the analysis (Baginski & Hassell, 1990). EFA techniques are more precise when every feature is denoted by several measured variables in the study. There should be as a minimum 3 to 5 measured variables per factor (Emami et al., 2012).

4.3.2.3.2 Fitting procedures

Fitting procedures are utilized to guess the factor loadings and unique variances of the model (*Factor loadings* are the regression coefficients among items and factors and measure the influence of a shared factor on a computed variable). There are a number of factor analysis matching techniques to select from, nonetheless there is not much evidence on each of their strengths and flaws. Principal axis factoring (PAF) and maximum likelihood (ML) are two extraction techniques that are commonly suggested. In general, ML or PAF provide the finest outcomes, subject to whether numbers are normally-distributed or if the notion of normality has been infringed (Baginski & Hassell, 1990).

4.3.2.3.3 Maximum Likelihood

The maximum likelihood technique has several advantages in that it permits scientists to calculate of an extensive range of indexes of the goodness of fit of the model, it lets scientists to examine the statistical importance of factor loadings, compute relationships amongst elements and calculate confidence intervals for these factors (Knauer & Wömpener, 2011). ML is the finest selection when data are normally distributed since "it permits for the calculation of a wide variety of indexes of the goodness of fit of the model and allows statistical significance testing of factor loadings and correlations among factors and the calculation of confidence intervals (Knauer & Wömpener, 2011). ML should not be employed if the data are not normally distributed.

4.3.2.3.4 Principal *axis factoring* (PAF)

Called "principal" axis factoring since the first factor accounts for as much shared variance as feasible, then the second factor next most variance, and so on. PAF is a explanatory technique so it is finest to use when the emphasis is only on your sample and you do not intend to generalize the outcomes further than your sample (Fabrigar, Wegener, MacCallum, & Strahan, 1999). A benefit of PAF is that it can be employed when the supposition of normality has been disrupted (Knauer & Wömpener, 2011). Another benefit of PAF is that it is less probable than ML to make wrong answers (Emami et al., 2012).

Following Rogers and Stocken (2005),the Difficulty latent variable is estimated by using the Principal Axis Factoring (PAF). The reason for using PAF is that some of the variables for estimating difficulty are dummy and therefore do not follow the normal distribution.

By using a number of indicators that represent the difficulty in forecasting, factor analysis was used to calculate the difficulty.

Table 4-3 reports result of the factor analysis when the continuous indicators of forecast difficulty are winsorized at 1 and 99 per cent levels.

Table 4-3. Correlation matrices and factor loadings for forecast difficulty measure

Panel A: Correlation Matrix for Forecast Difficulty Indicators

	STD-AF	STD-AFE	Lag-loss	Predict-loss	STD-Ret	Spread
STD-AF		0.001	0.033*	0.052*	0.330**	0.001
STD-AFE	-0.001		-0.031	-0.075	0.970**	0.320**
Lagged-loss	-0.014	0.144**		0.104**	-0.036	0.051*
Predict-loss	0.077**	0.050	0.104**		-0.054	-0.050
STD-Ret	0.330**	0.954**	0.171**	-0.029		0.954**
Spread	0.019	0.740**	0.188**	0.160**	0.748**	

Panel B: Factor Loadings

Indicator	STD-AF	STD-AFE	Lag-loss	Predict-loss	STD-Ret	Spread
Factor Lording	0.065	0.997	0.015	-0.021	0.997	0.118
Standardized Factor Score	0.039	0.958	0.112	-0.39	0.954	0.854

Panel C: Test of appropriateness of factor analysis

Total Variance Explained	68.30%		Chi-Square	50690
Kaiser-Meyer-Olkin Measure of Sampling Adequacy	0.620	Bartlett's Test of Sphericity	Sig.	0.000**

*, ** Significant at 5% and 1% level respectively.

All of the significant correlations among the indicators have their expected sign.

The Standard factor analysis heuristics (e.g., scree-plots and eigenvalues) suggested three factors, and after considering the sign and the magnitude of the factor loadings (shown in the appendix i), I extract the first factor as a amount of forecast complexity.

The values for difficulty ranges from -0.58 to 0.84, where the lower values of the variable characterize less difficulty, whereas higher values characterize a greater difficulty.

Kaiser-Meyer-Olkin (KMO) measure of sampling sufficiency is utilized to evaluate the extents of the seen correlation coefficients regarding the extents of the incomplete correlation coefficients. Large KMO amounts are pleasant as correlations between pairs of variables (i.e. partial factors) can be explained by the other variables. According to the Kaiser (1974) KMO values which are above 0.5 are acceptable.

Bartlett's test of sphericity is used in factor analysis to determine whether the correlations between the variables, examined simultaneously, do not differ significantly from zero. Factor analysis is usually conducted when the test is significant indicating that the correlations do differ from zero.

To see the appropriateness of the factor analysis Kaiser-Meyer-Olkin Measure of Sampling Adequacy have been calculated and Bartlett's Test of Sphericity have been performed. As reported in panel C of Table 4-3, the Bartlett's test of sphericity is significant at 0.000 level, which indicates that the factor analysis is appropriate (Bartlett, 1954). The KMO index is 0.620 (higher than 0.50), which indicates that the factor analysis is appropriate.

The next section presents the logistic regression models that test the relationship of analysts' recommendations and FM (H1), and the analysts' recommendations and FEs (H2).

4.3.3 Models

4.3.3.1 *The relationship of analysts' recommendations and forecast management (H1)*

The first hypothesis will be tested by running the regression of FM on AR, including moderators (Learning effect and Difficulty) and several control variables that the reason for using and measurement process of them are explained in the following paragraphs.

$$Prob(Down=1) = F(\alpha_0 + \alpha_1\ AR + \alpha_2 AR \times Difficulty + \alpha_3 AR \times FREQ + \alpha_4\ LMV + \alpha_5\ MB + \alpha_6\ Hightech + \alpha_7\ Lag\_Loss + \alpha_8 Year + \varepsilon)$$

$$(4\text{-}13)$$

Where,

AR = the Analysts' recommendations that takes the value of 1 to 5 (table 4-1)

$Difficulty$ = Difficulty to asses the credibility of managers' forecasts.

$FREQ$ = Frequency of FM in the previous four years as index of learning effect

LMV = Logarithm of market value

MB = Market to Book value

$Hightech$ = 1 if the firm is in one of the high technology industries such as pharmaceuticals, aircraft and spacecraft, medical, precision and optical instruments, radio, television and communication equipment, office, accounting and computing machinery, or zero otherwise.

Lag_loss = 1 when a firm's quarterly earnings report preceding the forecast is negative and 0 otherwise.

$Year$ = 1 if the firm-year is in 2010 and 0 otherwise.

Taking a page out of Rakow (2010), I converted LMV, MB and indicator variables that are set to one, if the value of the original variable is greater than or equal to the sample median, or zero otherwise.

Other control variable is the threat of litigation. Soffer et al. (2000) state that firms in a litigious environment want to prevent a large disappointment in the earnings announcement date (see Soffer et al. 2000), and this might be better accomplished by providing a less optimistic or even pessimistic forecast shortly before the earnings release date.

Kasznik and Lev (1995) posit that firms in high-tech industries face higher risk of litigation as they experience, larger price fluctuations, which might translate into potential losses to investors. Similarly, Baginski et al. (2002) uses high-tech industries to control potential firm-specific litigation risk. The earnings of high-tech firms are more volatile and inherently carry greater risks of inaccurate forecasts; all these factors could affect a firm's cost of capital. Therefore, a negative coefficient is predicted vis-à-vis high-tech, implying that high technology firms issue less optimistic forecasts.

Using dummy variables instead of continuous variable allows α_1 in equation (4-13) to be interpreted as the effect of independent variable when the dummy variable is equal to zero, while α_6 through α_8 can be interpreted as the effect of each variables when the dummy variable is equal to one.

For improving the robustness of the results, additional tests will be conducted, which includes tests such as ANOVA in order to compare difference of means of both buy and sell companies.

H2 is tested by running the following logit regression:

$$Prob(meet=1) = F(\alpha_0 + \alpha_1\,AR + \alpha_2\,FREQ + \alpha_3\,Difficulty + \alpha_4\,LMV + \alpha_5\,MB + \alpha_6 DA + \alpha_7\,Hightech + \alpha_8\,Lag\text{-}loss + \alpha_9\,Year + \varepsilon)$$
$$(4\text{-}14)$$

Where,

FE is represented by *meet* variable, which equals 1 if a firm's actual earnings meets or exceeds the management's forecasts, or 0 otherwise.

DA is the firm's ability to manipulate earnings, as reflected by its discretionary accruals, which makes it ideal as a control. I use a version of the cross-sectional modified Jones model which is used by Bergstresser and Philippon (2006) to estimate discretionary accruals. Other independent and control variables are similar to what was explained for equation (4-13).

For testing H3 and H4, the ANOVA will be used to test the difference of mean value of FM between the companies that meet or miss forecasts in the buy and sell companies separately.

For testing H5 and H6, after removing (deducting) value of forecasts management from the issued forecast[1], forecasts[2] errors are calculated using nonbiased forecasts and reported forecasts. Then, chi-square test will be used to test the differences in the occurrences of positive FEs between FEs that are calculated by using unbiased forecasts (unmanaged FEs) and FEs that are calculated by using issued forecasts.

4.3.3.2 *Analysis of Variance*

One-way analysis of variance (ANOVA) is a technique used to compare means of two or more samples (Howell, 2012). The ANOVA tests the null hypothesis that samples in two or more groups are pulled from populations with the identical mean values. To do this, two estimates are got of the population variance. The ANOVA creates an F-statistic, the ratio of the variance calculated amongst the averages to the variance inside the samples. If the group means are pulled from populations with the same mean values, the variance among the group means would be lesser than

---

[1] Following the methodology of (Gleason & Mills, 2008) the reported forecast is decomposed into the management and unmanaged component. The unmanaged forecast is defined as the difference between the reported forecast and the managed component (Felleg et al., 2012).

the variance of the samples, following the central limit theorem. A upper ratio therefore suggests that the samples were drained from populations with dissimilar mean values (Howell, 2012). These estimates rely on various assumptions.

- Response variable are normally distributed (or approximately normally distributed).
- Samples are independent.

in order to obtain better comparison of forecasts management (H1) between buy and sell companies, the differences of means of forecasts management measure ($FM\_Mutsomoto$), between buy and sell companies are tested in section 5.2.3.1.2.

4.3.4 Data and Sample

4.3.4.1 *Unit of Analysis*

Unit of analysis explains the level of analysis where information regarding the research is collected (Zikmund, 2003). Although determining the unit of analysis is very simple, it is very critical to ascertain the unit of analysis on the threshold of the study. The reason is that the determination of the variables for the theoretical model, sample size, suitable data collection approaches are reliant on the unit of analysis (Zikmund, 2003). This study chose the firm-year as the unit of analysis.

4.3.4.2 *Data Collection*

The company's stock trading information, along with the forecast data, is collected from the Bloomberg database. The potential market that was considered for data collection is companies in the New York Stock Exchange (NYSE).

The analysts provide financial information to investors, contributing to the efficiency of the market. In smaller stock exchanges, there are comparably less analysts, and therefore useful information is less available to investors. Numerous analysts analyse companies in NYSE. According to Li and Ding (2010), Castura et al. (2010), and Correia et al. (2005), the NYSE is semi-strongly efficient. Since this research considers stock characteristics as an incentive that affects the quality of accounting information, semi-strong efficiency is a prerequisite for testing the hypotheses, and since NYSE is a relatively large and efficient market, it will be taken into account in this research.

The other reason for considering NYSE is that many analysts are active in the NYSE market. This creates large samples of analysts' recommendations, which makes the generalization of the result of this research more convenient.

The years of 2009-2010 are chosen for sample period. The reason the sample was not extended to previous years is that the year 2008 was not an optimum year for most equity investors

(Longstaff, 2010). Although most financial analysts had anticipated the appreciation in stock, and subsequently derivative markets, they unexpectedly experience depreciation in the markets. In fact, the financial/credit crisis caused a downturn in consumer and business spending in the year, which were subsequently reflected in equity markets.

According to Longstaff (2000) the subprime crisis brought about an almost complete halt to the fledgling structured-credit market, a serious credit crunch for both individuals and financial institutions, and a major decline in the liquidity of debt securities in virtually every market. Longstaff (2010) explains the stages over which the shocks in the credit market spill over into the stock market. He explains that when contagion occurs the negative returns in the credit market affect subsequent returns in other markets like the stock market.

For example, some of the effects on the stock market were that, due to the external and internal economic events, US indices abruptly declined in the year. The Dow Jones Index (DJI) experienced a decline of around 35%, and the S&P 500 and tech laden Nasdaq (IXIC) indices dropped to near 40% during the year. Following the stock market crash and dramatic decline (s) in stock prices, the Business Week Journal (Mandel 2008) on October 10, 2008, described the existing market condition as the stock market meltdown, and called it the "Panic of 2008". Therefore, the sudden fall in stock prices in 2008 resulted in significant losses for the markets participants. This downward trend of US stock market was to some extent, reversed in the year 2009.

4.3.5 The Crisis Effect

The reason the sample was not extended to previous years is that, due to credit crisis there was uncertainty in the U.S. financial market. Such uncertainty would have affected the quality of both managers' forecasts (which acts as my dependent variable) and the quality of the analysts' recommendations (which acts as my independent variable). Such effects will be explained in the following sections.

4.3.5.1 *How the Crisis Affect the Managers' Forecast*

Shivakumar, Urcan, Vasvari, & Zhang (2011) explain that, how the credit crisis increased the information uncertainty in the stock market. Kim, Pandit & Wasley (2012), examine the role macroeconomic uncertainty plays in influencing managers' decision to issue management earning forecasts as well as the characteristics of the forecasts that get issued. They find that, the level of market-wide uncertainty affects the characteristics of forecasts. Managers shift to earnings preannouncements and to shorter-horizon, but more precise forecasts. In addition, they find that firms with higher litigation risk increase earnings guidance when market uncertainty is high, presumably to shield themselves from legal liability.

In addition, Kim, Pandit, & Wasley (Xu, 2010) find that during periods of high market-level uncertainty, managers tend to issue more neutral news forecasts and they reduce bad news forecasts. Similarly, Shivakumar et al. (2011), present that, the significance of managers' forecasts to credit markets is chiefly altered in periods of high insecurity, as experienced during the recent credit crisis. The reason might be that, according to Epstein & Schneider (2008), Lang (1991), Shivakumar et al. (2011) and Veronesi (1999) market reactions to information vary depending on the level of information uncertainty.

The following section explains the effect of crisis on the analysts' recommendations.

4.3.5.2 *How the Crisis Affect the Analysts' Rrecommendations*

According to Kelly and Ljungqvist (2012) and Hong and Kacperczyk (2010),there have been significant amount of both broker closures and broker mergers during the financial crisis. Such broker closures and broker mergers cause analysts to be terminated and analyst coverage to decrease for the firms hitherto covered by these analysts.

In addition, Derrien & Kecskés (2013) shows that decrease in analyst coverage increases information asymmetry. Therefore, as a result of reduction in analyst following stock prices decrease substantially and thus the cost of capital would be increased. Such increase in the cost of capital increases the cost of external funding both in absolute terms and in relation to the cost of internal funding, the ideal extent of external financing decreases as well. In summary, a decrease in analyst coverage leads to a reduction in investment and financing. Thus, the decrease in analyst following causes firms to switch to funding that is less subtle to information asymmetry such reduction in the investment and funding will considerably influence the corporate reporting policies.

To avoid the noise of meddling of the effects of financial crises, the sample was not extended to the previous years[1] . On the other hand, since Matsumoto (2002) documented that the tendency of avoiding negative earnings surprises tend to increase over time, the most recent available data was chosen for analysis in order to avoid obsolete/unusable results. Therefore, I expect to discover significant results by concentrating on the available data of latest years (i.e. 2009-10). The total number of companies that traded their stocks on AMEX in NYSE is 2833. Due to the difficulty in

3

---

[1] In order to evaluate the reliability of the results on longer time periods, the researcher tested the hypotheses using all firm years between 2005 and 2010. The results showed that except for the second hypothesis that was accepted, there are no significant difference between the crisis and the non-crisis periods. However, since the sample of 2009 and 2010 firm-years are big enough and are on the safe side, we present the interpretations on the basis of the results of the years 2009 and 2010 in order to avoid distorting the effect of crisis. The results of the analysis on the basis of longer time periods (2005-2010) are available based on requests.

interpreting their accruals (Desai, Rajgopal, & Venkatachalam, 2004; Riley, 2007), the financial companies will be omitted from the sample.

4.4   Characteristics of the Data

The Bloomberg database is used to identify 5666 annual financial statements that are released between January 2009 and December 2010. From this number of companies, the AR for 4489 companies were available (table 2). The sample selection procedure is summarized in Table 4-4.

Table 4-4. Sampling procedure

Number of all company-years in NYSE (2009-10)		5666
Less: Companies that their AR are not available		(1177)
Number of the companies for which AR is available (Table 4-3)		4489
Less: Utilities, transportation or financial service	423	
Forecasts are not available	285	
Forecasts issued less than one month prior to the end of fiscal year	580	
Insufficient data to calculate standard deviation of analysts' forecasts	192	
Missing data for control variables on Bloomberg	104	
Insufficient time-series data on Bloomberg	237	
Forecasts that are not in quarter 4	92	
		(1913)
Sample company-years for testing hypotheses		2576

Since firms in regulated industries are more likely to have different incentives than non-regulated firms (Matsumoto, 2002), regulated industries including utilities, transportation companies, and financial services companies are excluded from the sample.

There are a total of 285 company-years with unavailable forecast in the Bloomberg database, while there are 580 company-years with forecasts issued within a month prior to the fiscal year end. These company-years were dismissed to avoid including preannouncements (Rogers and Stocken 2005).

For 192 company-years, few analysts' are actually following the information of the firms, which renders the determination of the analysts' forecasts standard deviation unreliable. For 104 of the company-years, data for calculation of control variables are unavailable. Two hundred thirty seven Companies with insufficient data for earnings managements' calculation, which is another control variable, are also excluded. Finally, among the remaining company-years for 92 companies, the forecasts for the fourth quarter are unavailable.

Among the remaining company-years, the Bloomberg database was searched for management earnings estimates, and actual (realized) earnings. The database was also searched for data regarding the analysts' recommendations, along with other relevant financial data pertaining to this work.

Based on the availability of the aforementioned data and in order to conduct prediction tests that involve examining forecasts reactions to analysts' recommendations, a subsample of 2576 forecasts was used.

4.4.1 Multivariate Assumptions

Multivariate analysis needs several suppositions to be met. Breaches from assumption can lead to a number of difficulties which ranges from mistaken results of significantly wrong and biased coefficients predications of the hypothesized associations (Hair, Black, Babin, Anderson, & Tatham, 2006).

4.4.1.1 *Normality*

Normality is applied to define a curve that is bell-shaped and symmetrical. The maximum score frequency is shown in the midpoint with lower frequencies near to the edges.

Normality can be settled by measuring the variables levels of skewness or kurtosis. According to Hair et al. (2006), if the value of skew or kurtosis (ignoring any minus sign) is more than twice the standard error, then the distribution is meaningfully different from a normal distribution. However, concern of non-normality should not be any problem here because of the study's large sample size (n>200). Hair et al. (2006) highlighted that for sample sizes of 200 or more, the "detrimental effect of non-normality" is negligible (p. 80). However, for purpose of realizing the extent to which normality distribution is assumed in the sample, results are analysed.

4.4.2 Outliers

Outliers are instances that have out-of-range values as compared to the bulk of other instances. The existence of outliers in the data may mislead statistical test result. Outliers can be detected from the residual scatter plot. However, a small number of outliers in big samples are common and most of the time, taking any action is not required (Hair et al. 2006).

Following Rogers and Stocken (2005) to avoid the effect of outliers, the data was winsorized at the top and bottom 1 per cent.

4.4.3 Multicollinearity

Multicollinearity mean there is extreme intercorrelations amongst the independent variables. In examining relationships between independent and dependent variables, the incidence of Multicollinearity can produce several problems including imprecise outcomes of regression coefficient approximation. One of the ways to check for the incidence of multicollinearity in the data is by measuring the tolerance and the variance inflation factor. Tolerance is a value that measures the degree of the independent variables variability that is not explained by the other independent variables in the model. Variance inflation factor (VIF) is the opposite of Tolerance and is computed merely by overturning the tolerance value. An sign of multicollinearity is when the value of

Tolerance is less than 0.10 and VIF is more than 10 (Hair et al., 2006).

As suggested by Hair et al. (2006), multicollinearity among independent variables can be assessed by the VIF values caused from the analysis of standard multiple regressions among the independent and dependent variables. Remedies for multicollinearity troubles should be taken if the VIF value shows more than 10.

As mentioned in the previous chapter, and following the previous literature, control variables are included in the analysis of the relationship between analysts' recommendation, forecasts management and forecasts errors in the following sections to analyse the relationship in the presence of difficulty and frequency.

4.5   Summary

In this chapter, following Abarbanell and Lehavy(2003b) and Dutta and Gigler (2002), it was hypothesised that the stocks recommended by analysts to sell (sell companies) presented non-growth companies that are unable to conduct earnings management, and therefore, in order to produce positive earnings surprise, they subscribed to downward biased forecasts strategy. However, the stocks that analysts recommend to buy (buy companies) are representing growth companies that possesses profitable investment opportunities, and their future news are highly followed by investors, which can effectively conduct income increasing earnings management. Furthermore, after explaining the procedures that have been used to calculate the research variables, the chapter discussed the statistical techniques that are used to test the hypotheses. Finally, the chapter concludes with explaining the data and sample of the research.

Chapter 5. FINDINGS

5.1 Introduction

The discussion of the findings in this study will be presented in this chapter. Firstly, this chapter presents the descriptive statistics of the variables. After presenting the descriptive statistics that are related to the sample, this chapter presents the analysis of the results related to the relationship of analysts recommendation and forecasts management. On top of that, the initial tests on the relationship, as per the analysts' recommendations, forecasts management and forecasts errors will also be presented. Finally, the logistic regression is used to include control and moderating variables of the learning effect and difficulty. All hypotheses testing are conducted in the two samples collected from all companies involved, and also from the companies that have near-zero forecasts errors. To remind the reader, the following paragraphs restate the research questions, hypotheses that fit into them and the statistical procedures that applied to answer each question.

The analysis of the relationship of analyst's recommendation and forecasts management is in relation to the first research question which states "Does the management of sell companies produce more downward biased forecasts than the management of buy companies?"

179

In relation to the first question, the hypothesis 1 (H1) states that, "buy companies issue less pessimistic (i.e., more informative) forecasts than sell companies". In other words, sell companies issue more pessimistic (less informative) forecasts than the buy companies.

In order to answer the first research question and test the H1, chi-square is used to test whether sell companies issue more pessimistic forecasts than buy companies. In addition, the analysis of variance is used to test the difference in the mean of forecasts management of the buy and sell companies. Finally, in the logistic regression analysis, a number of control variables are included to test the relationship of analysts' recommendations and forecasts management.

The second research question is "Does the management of sell companies have higher positive forecasts errors than the management of buy companies?" To address the research question 2, Hypothesis 2 (H2) states that, Sell companies have higher frequency of positive forecasts errors than buy companies.

To answer the second research question, chi-square is used to test the differences in frequency of positive forecasts errors between buy and sell companies. In addition, analysis of variance is used to test the difference of the mean forecasts errors between the buy and sell companies. Finally, in the logistic regression analysis, a number of control variables are included to test the relationship of the analysts' recommendations and forecasts errors.

The rest of the chapter answers the third research question which states "Does the management of sell companies produce more downward biased forecasts to achieve positive forecasts errors than the management of buy companies?"

Hypothesis 3 (H3) states that, in sell companies, those that meet forecasts are more likely to do income decreasing FM than companies that do not meet forecasts.

To test the hypothesis 3, analysis of variance is used to test the significance of difference in mean FM for companies that meet the forecasts and the companies that miss the forecasts in the sell companies.

Hypothesis 4 (H4) states that, there is no significant difference in income decreasing FM between buy companies that meet forecasts and those that do not meet forecasts.

To test the H4, analysis of variance is used to test the significance of difference in mean FM for companies that meet the forecasts and the companies that miss the forecasts in the buy companies.

Hypothesis 5 (H5) states that, For sell companies, the frequency of positive forecasts errors is expected to decrease when forecasts errors are based on "unmanaged" rather than issued forecasts.

To test the hypothesis 5, chi-square is used to test the frequency of positive forecasts errors between forecasts errors that are calculated using "unmanaged" and issued forecasts in the sell side companies.

Hypothesis 6 (H6) states that, for buy companies, incidence of positive forecasts errors is not expected to decrease when forecasts errors are based on "unmanaged" rather than issued forecasts.

To test the hypothesis 6, contingency table is used to test the frequency of positive forecasts errors between forecasts errors that are calculated using unmanaged and issued forecasts in the buy side companies.

The next section presents the characteristics of the data.

5.2 Findings

Descriptive statistics such as minimum, maximum, means, standard deviation, median, skewness and kurtosis were obtained for the interval-scaled dependent and independent variables. The software of SPSS Statistics 18.0 was employed for this purpose.

The descriptive statistics for forecasts revisions, errors, management and analysts' recommendations are shown in **Error! R eference source not found.**.

Table 5 1. Descriptive statistics for independent variable, proxies for incentives to avoid negative earnings surprises, and control variables

Variables	Mean	Standard deviation	1st Quartile	Median	3rd Quartile	Skewness
Dependent Variables						
FE	-0.00011	0.000915	-0.00019	-0.00001	0.00003	-0.00122
FM_Matsumoto	-0.00951	0.001049	-0.00401	-0.00182	-0.00052	0.000246
Independent Variable						
AR	3.816	0.527	3.444	3.857	4.200	0.015
Control Variables						
Diff	-0.02083	0.055673	-0.03485	-0.01792	0.01735	-0.06446
Freq	0.726355	0.663353	0	1	1	
LMV	9.100301	0.792903	8.536527	9.172754	9.634178	-0.01133
MB	1.547844	0.476359	1.15	1.729001	2.800003	-0.33807
STD_Ret	9.047587	1.562583	8.879559	9.881865	11.03039	0.43207
STD_AF	0.280425	0.443315	0.029829	0.102086	0.290273	0.42355
DA	-0.00887	0.161277	-0.04403	0.000084	0.039199	-0.21503
Spread	0.016223	0.31589	0.000044	0.000212	0.001128	0.05638

As proven in **Error! Reference source not found.**, the m ean and the median of the measure of forecasts management (*FM_Matsumoto*) are negative. That is in line with the findings of Kasznik (1995), which state that companies generally engage in negative forecast management for the purpose of meeting or beating the forecasts.

The first and third quartiles value of -0.004082 and-0.000525 explains that most of the companies have negative forecast management. The skewness value of 0.٠0٠٢٤٦ proves a positive skew of distribution to the right. Furthermore, the negative kurtosis value of -0.001476 points to a curve that is less peaked than the normal distribution. Accordingly, it can be concluded that distribution is reasonably normal.

The mean and median value for the variable *FE* are -0.00011and -0.00001 respectively (**Error! Reference source not f ound.**) which indicates that the overall extent of negative forecasts errors is larger than positive forecasts errors, while the standard deviation is 0.000915. The third quartile value of 0.00003 shows that there are some companies which have positive forecasts errors. The negative value of skewness-0.00122 shows a negligible skew of distribution to the left. In addition, the positive value of kurtosis 0.00137 is a sign of a curve that is faintly more peaked than the normal distribution. Therefore, it can be concluded that distribution is logically normal.

The analysts' recommendations vary from 1 to 5. The mean analysts' recommendation is 3.816, and the median of the analysts' recommendation is 3.875, which indicates that the greater percentages of the companies are sell side companies.

5.2.1   Initial Tests

Before reporting the findings of the main tests of hypotheses, the findings of initial tests, including tests of correlations and graphs of forecasts management are duly reported.

As explained in the previous chapter, the measure of forecasts management which is used in this study is *FM_Matsumoto*. Table 5-1 presents the correlation coefficients among management's forecasts management measure (*FM_Matsumoto*), management's forecasts errors (i.e. the difference between managers' forecasts and actual earnings), and the analysts' recommendations. In the correlation table, the *FM* measure is considered as a binary variable, in which $FM\_Matsumoto = 1$ if $FM\_Matsumoto < 0$ and *FM_Matsumoto* =0 otherwise. Similarly, FE is also considered as binary variables, in which *FE=1* if FE is either zero or positive and *FE=0* otherwise. As it is evident in Table 5-1, there are positive correlations between FE and the measure of FM According to Burgestahler and Eams (2002), due to the management considering the cost of managing forecasts to be exorbitantly high, they limit

the magnitude of forecasts managements to a small level. In

Table 5-1. Correlations matrix.

Pearson correlations appear below diagonal for all companies, above diagonal for the companies in small distance around zero forecast error

	AR	FE	FM_Matsumoto	Difficulty	Freq	AR*Difficulty	AR*Freq
AR		0.104**	0.131**	0.041	0.005	0.008	0.187**
FE	-0.108		0.242**	0.352**	0.429**	0.324**	0.000
FM_Matsumoto	0.077**	0.030*		0.074*	0.114**	0.049	-0.074**
Difficulty	-0.47	0.000	-0.016		0.701**	0.969**	-0.663**
Freq	0.084	0.248**	-0.14	-0.061**		-0.684**	0.957**
AR*Difficulty	-0.033*	0.001	-0.013	0.699**	0.139**		-0.683**
AR*Freq	0.354**	0.201**	0.042**	-0.055**	0.914**	-0.139**	

*, ** Significant at 0.05 and 0.01

AR = Analysts' Recommendations.

FE = is the forecast Error.

FM_Matsumoto = is the measure of forecasts management which is calculated through using parameters that are obtained from prior firm-years. (FM_Matsumoto is set to 1 if FM measure (FM_Matsumoto) is negative and 0 otherwise)

Difficulty = Reflects how much it is difficult for the market participants to assess the credibility of management's forecasts

FREQ= is the frequency of forecasts management in the previous years

According to Burgestahler and Eams (2002), due to the management considering the cost of managing forecasts to be exorbitantly high, they limit the magnitude of forecasts managements to a small level. In addition the benefit of beating forecasts by a high extent and producing large positive FE is only marginally higher than just meeting the forecasts and producing small positive FE. Therefore, hypotheses testing were conducted on two subsamples of all of the companies (first subsample) and the companies that have small positive FEs (second subsample). Table 5-1 presents the correlation of the variables in two

186

subsamples of all of the companies, and second for the companies that have near-zero FEs.

The negative correlation of *FE* with *AR* (Analysts' recommendations) is consistent with the work reported by Dutta and Gigler (2003) and Abarbanell and Lehavy (2003b), who believe that buy-companies conduct income increasing earnings management to meet or beat forecasts. The significant positive correlations between AR and *FM_Matsumoto* confirms that sell-companies do income-decreasing forecasts management.

Pallant (2005, p. 150) suggests that a commonly used cut-off points for determining the presence of multicollinearity is a tolerance value of less than 0.1, or a Variance Inflation Factor (VIF) value of more than 10. The VIF for the independent variables are indicated in Table 5-2, which indicates an absence of high correlation between independent variables.

Table 5-2. Variance Inflation Factor for the companies near zero FE

Variables	AR_Freq	AR_Diff	Lag_loss	Year	AR	LMV	High_Tech	MB	Mean VIF
VIF	2.87	2.78	1.27	1.21	1.19	1.1	1.02	1.01	1.56

5.2.1.1 *The relationship of analysts' recommendations and forecasts management*

Figure 5-1 represents measure of forecasts management (FM_Matsumoto) against *AR*.

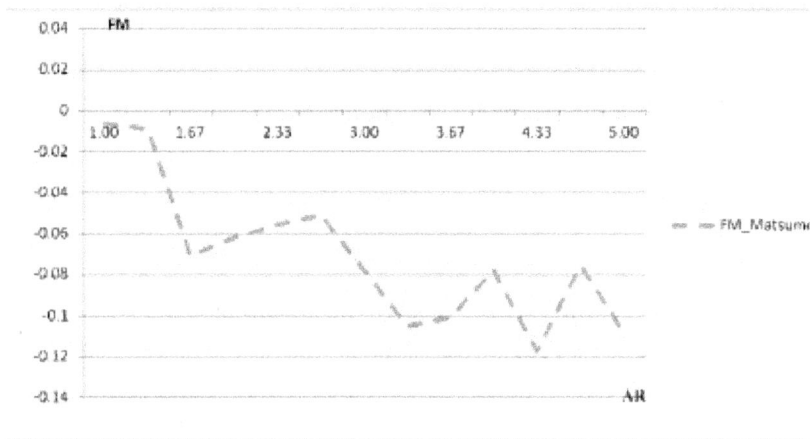

Figure 5-1. The graph of*FM_Matsumoto* on Analysts'
Recommendations (AR).
All measures are multiplied by 10 for ease of
presentation. The analysts' recommendations vary
from 1 to 5 whereas 5 = Strong sell, 4= Sell, 3= Hold,
2= Buy and 1 = Strong buy.

Figure 5-1shows that sell-companies perform more downward forecasts revision than buy-companies. The graph shows that most of the companies do downward forecasts revision, which is consistent with the theories discussed by Wang (2003) and Lim (2001); when there is long horizon, managers are initially optimistic and manage their forecasts downward afterward.

According to $FM\_Matsumoto$ graph in Figure 5-1, sell companies do more downward forecasts management compared to buy companies. However, a number of more accurate techniques will be used to test the differences of $FM_{Matsumoto}$ between buy and sell-companies. The next sections present some more accurate techniques that have been used to test the differences in the measures of FM and FE in the buy and sell companies.

The next sections describe the findings of the hypotheses testing.

5.2.2 Main Tests

Burgstahler and Eames (2002) argued that the benefit of forecast management to a firm may increase of the amount of forecast management, i.e. there may be incremental benefits to beating rather than just meeting analyst forecasts. However, forecast management also imposes a cost on the firm. Among such costs would be management bad reputation for inaccurate reporting (Graham et al., 2005; Hair et al., 2006). For example

Ettredgeet al. (2011) state that forecast bias will cause the management to lose reputation. Such loss of reputation could be a kind of cost that management incurs as a result of doing forecasts management.

If there is a sudden drop in the marginal benefit at the point just to the right of the zero surprise point for many firms, then zero surprise is the optimal level a firm should achieve by conducting forecast management. Realistically, this scenario is entirely possible. The benefit(s) to firms to just meet expectations is much larger than that for firms just failing to meet expectations by a small margin, whereas the benefit to firms that beat the expectations is only marginally larger than that of firms that just meet the expectations. This argument implies that firms that just meet expectations are more likely to conduct forecast management compared to firms that just fail to meet expectations and firms that just beat expectations.

Therefore, the main statistical tests are divided into two parts. In the first part, the hypotheses are tested by taking into consideration all of the involved company-years (first subsample). In the second part, the hypotheses are tested by considering the company-years that are in the vicinity of zero forecasts errors (second subsample).

The first subsample was 2576 company-years. The second subsample was 1303 company-years.

5.2.3 Analysis of First Subsample

5.2.3.1 *Relationship of Analysts' Recommendation and Forecasts Management (H1)*

Sell companies are expected to have more pessimistic (less optimistic) forecasts management. Therefore, the research hypothesis is presented as follows:

H1: Sell companies issue more pessimistic forecasts than buy companies.

The study tests the proposed relationship of analysts' recommendations and forecasts management by using the contingency table.

5.2.3.1.1 Contingency table

Contingency table is essentially used to analyse and record the relationship between two or more categorical variables. A "categorical forecast" is a forecast of the happening or not happening of a particular incident, which should be openly described. In this test, I am interested in predicting whether or not the forecasts management is downward (*FM_Matsumoto* is negative) or forecasts management is upward (*FM_Matsumoto* is positive), the downward forecasts management will really happen or not. This leads to four possibilities as laid out in the Table 5-3. The values of the table are achieved by checking the number of times each of the four likely patterns of forecast and observed category happened.

In order to provide evidence that the analysts' recommendations do capture the incentive to conduct downward forecasts management to avoid negative earnings surprises, I examine the relation between: (1) the analysts' recommendations, and (2) the forecasts management (DOWN). Table 5-3 presents the Chi-square test.

Table 5-3. Association between analysts' recommendations and downward forecasts managements for all of the companies.

Contingency table classifying firm-years based on (1) stock transaction status, and (2) sign of forecasts management		proxies for forecasts management	
		FM_Matsumoto	
		Positive (Down =0)	Negative (Down=1)
Number of firm-years (% of firm years conditional on Buy or Sell	Sell	27.38% 674	72.62% 1792
	Buy	32.11% 255	67.89% 564
Pearson Chi-square		$\chi 2= 4.2$ $P=0.041$	

The third and fourth columns summarize the relation between stock transaction status and forecasts management (*DOWN*). The

Chi-square analysis showed that, the sell-companies have higher frequency of negative *FM_Matsumoto* compared to buy companies, with the differences being significant at 0.05 levels. The Chi-Square value is 4.2. Table 5-3 indicates that sell-companies have higher frequency of negative forecasts management compared to buy companies. This supports the H1.

5.2.3.1.2 **Analysis of Variance**

In order to make sure that the assumptions of ANOVA hold, I explain them in the following paragraphs.

According to Hair et al. (2006), if the value of Skew or Kurtosis (ignoring any minus sign) is larger than twofold the standard error, then the distribution considerably varies from a normal distribution. Nevertheless, concerns of non-normality is not a concern at this point due to the study's big sample size (n>200). Hair et al. (2006) highlighted that for sample sizes of 200 or more, the "detrimental effect of non-normality" is insignificant (p. 80). However, for aim of comprehending the degree to which normality distribution is supposed in the sample, results regarding the distribution of the sample are analysed.

As reported in **Error! Reference source not found.**, it is evident that the measures of Skewness and Kurtosis are -0.00122 and 0.00137 for *FE* and 0.000246 and -0.0147 for *FM_Matsumoto* respectively. According to **Error! Reference source not found.**, t he standard deviation for the FE and FM_Matsumoto are 0.000915 and 0.001049 respectively. Since none of the values of Skewness and Kurtosis for FE and FM_Matsumoto are higher than twice of their respective standard deviations, it is concluded that the distribution of *FE* and *FM_Matsumoto* are normal. Therefore, the first assumption for ANOVA is met. The second assumption for Analysis of Variance is also met as the sample of buy and sell companies are independent.

Next, in order to obtain better comparison of forecasts management (H1) between buy and sell companies, the differences of means of forecasts management measure (*FM_Mutsomoto*), between buy and sell companies are tested.

Table 5-4. Test of comparison of means of **FM** among companies that have been classified into the groups of buy and sell, according to their value of **AR** (for all companies)

	N (Mean) FM_Matsumoto	Minimum (Maximum) FM_Matsumoto	STDEV FM_Matsumoto
Sell	2465 (-0.01026)	-0.03649 (0.0374)	0.00515
Buy	809 (-0.00258)	-0.02647 (0.0259)	0.00701
All	3274 (-0.00836)	-0.0365 (0.0374)	0.00606
Buy vs. sell	F 0.859	sig. 0.354	

In Table 5-4the difference of measure of forecasts management is not significant between the groups of buy and sell. The Table 5-4 indicates that, there is no significant difference in the forecasts management of the buy side and sell side companies.

As mentioned in the previous chapter, and following the previous literature, control and moderator variables are included in the analysis of the relationship between analysts' recommendation, forecasts management and forecasts errors in the following sections to analyse the relationship in the presence of difficulty and frequency. The next section explains running the regression in presence of the control variables.

5.2.3.1.3   **Control Variables for Testing the Relationship of Analysts' Recommendations and Forecasts Management**

Based on the findings of previous researches, a number of control variables should be considered when regressing forecasts management as dependent variable(s). This section explains the control variables that have been previously stated to significantly affect the management incentive to conduct forecasts management, while the moderator variables will be explained in the next section.

In addition to the incentives that are publicly observable, managers face the incentives to misrepresent their information that are indirectly observable, but are implicitly revealed through their forecasting behaviour; for instance, a manager's performance contract, which often is not publicly observable, may induce biased forecasting (Kim & Shi, 2011).

Numerous researches discover that forecast behaviour is related with a firm's size (Baginski and Hassell 1997; Bamber and Cheon 1998). The natural log of the firm's market capitalization one day earlier to the forecast; its denoted *LMV*, is utilized as a proxy for a firm's size. Bamber and Cheon (1998) documented that expansion prospects influence a firm's forecasting behaviour. They use a firm's market value to book value of equity ratio, M/B, as a measure of a firm's growth opportunities. M/B is computed as the share of the firm's market capitalization one day earlier to the forecast, divided by the preceding year's book value of equity. In addition, I included the lagged losses (Hayn 1995; Basu 1997).

The other control variable is the threat of litigation. Soffer et al. (2000) stated that that firms in a litigious environment want to prevent a large disappointment in the earnings announcement date (see Soffer et al. 2000). This goal might be better accomplished by providing a less optimistic or even pessimistic forecast, shortly before the earnings release date.

Kasznik and Lev (1995) posit that firms involved in the high-tech industries face greater risks of litigation, as they face larger price fluctuations that might result in potential losses to investors. Similarly, Baginski et al. (2002) uses the high-tech industry to control for potential firm-specific litigation risks. High-tech firms have added unpredictable profits and larger risk of imprecise predictions; all of these issues could influence a firm's cost of capital. Hence, a positive coefficient on High-tech is predicted, which means that most of the time, high-technology firms issue less optimistic (more pessimistic) forecasts.

In order to test the relationship of the analysts' recommendations and forecasts management in the presence of the aforementioned control variables, logistic regressions were used to regress measure of forecast managements against the analysts' recommendations. Table 5-5 reports the results for the logistic regression analysis of the FM (Equation 4-13).

Table 5-5. Results for the managers' forecast bias hypothesis (Hypothesis 1). Logistic regression results for the first subsample.

Model: $Prob(Down=1)=$
$F(a_0+a_1AR+a_2AR*Difficulty+a_3AR*Freq+a_4LMV+a_5MB+a_6Hightech+a_7Log\_loss+a_8Year)$

Dependent Variable: (Down=1) if FM_Matsumoto is negative and (Down=0) otherwise

Variable	Predicted sign	Coefficients	p-values	Marginal effects
Dependent		FM_Matsumoto	FM_Matsumoto	FM_Matsumoto
Independents				
Constant	?	1.034	0.276	-
AR	+	0.689	0.010**	1.993
Moderating Variables				
AR*Difficulty	+	3.250	0.003***	2.577
AR*Freq	-	-0.115	0.114	0.891
Control Variables				
LMV	+	0.155	0.422	1.167
MB	-	-0.006	0.654	0.994
High_Tech	+	-0.180	0.399	0.835
			0.044**	1.647
Log_Loss	+	0.499	0.000***	
Year	-	-1.162		0.145

Log Likelihood	564.693	**Hosmer Lemeshow**	
Chi-square	57.602	Pearson Chi	510.36
P-value	0.000	Prob	0.243

*, **, *** Significant at 0.1, 0.05 and 0.01 levels, respectively based on one-tailed tests for signed predictions, two-tailed tests otherwise

Control Variables:
LMV: the natural log of the firm's market capitalization one day preceding to the forecast
MB: firm's market value to book value of equity ratio
High_Tech: equals one, if the firm is in high technology industry and zero otherwise
Log_loss: indicates whether the company experienced loss in the previous period (Log_loss=0) or not (Log_loss=1)
Year: indicates whether the firm-year belongs to 2010 (year = 1) or belongs to 2009 (year = 0)

According to regression 4-13 which is restated on the top of Table 5-5, the interaction term of AR and historical frequency of earnings management ($Freq$) is used to measure the effect of learning from historical forecasts management on the relationship of *AR* and forecasts management. Thus, the algebraic expression for H1 is that a_l is positive. However, the algebraic expression of learning effect is that a_3 is negative and significant. In this specification, the coefficient of forecasts management to *AR* should be $a_l + a_3 \times$ *Freq.* Specifically, the coefficient of forecasts management to *AR* for a zero-time downward forecast management firm is exactly a_1. However, the coefficient of forecasts management to *AR* for a one-time downward forecast management firm is $a_1 + a_3$, and for a two-time downward forecast management firm, it is$a_1 + \alpha_3 \times 2$, while for a three-time downward forecast management firm, it is $\alpha_1 + \alpha_3 \times 3$.

A similar analysis is derived for difficulty. The coefficient of forecasts management to *AR* for a non-difficult firm is exactly a_1. However, the coefficient of forecasts management to *AR* for a difficult firm is $a_1 + a_2$.

Considering the content of Table 5-5, the coefficient of *AR* is positive and significant at a 0.05 level. The coefficients on *AR* × *Difficulty* is significantly positive. Thus, as a result of the significance of the coefficients of *AR*, it is concluded that *AR* is an independent variable. The difficulty moderates the relationship of *AR* and *FM_Matsumoto*. This result is consistent with the managers strategically manipulating their forecasts downward, when it is more difficult for the markets to assess the truthfulness of their disclosure. The coefficients of $AR \times Freq$ is not significant.

Regarding the control variables, the coefficients of lag_Loss is significantly positive, meaning that the companies that are experiencing lagged loss do more downward forecasts management compared to other companies. The coefficient of the year is also significantly negative. This means that in 2009, the companies do more downward forecasts management than in 2010. The coefficients on the remaining control variables are insignificant.

The Hosmer and Lemeshow test were used to test the fitness of the models. The test result shown in the lower part of Table 5-5 is insignificant, which confirms the goodness of fit of the model.

The VIF statistics for my variables are indicated in Table 5-6, which indicates no sign of high correlation between independent variables.

Table 5-6. Variance Inflation Factor for all of the companies

Variab les	AR_Fr eq	AR_D iff	Lag_l oss	Yea r	AR	LM V	High_T ech	M B	Me an VIF
VIF	1.7	1.45	1.28	1.1 4	1.1 1	1.0 5	1.01	1	1.2 2

5.2.3.2 *Relationship of Analysts' recommendations and Forecasts Errors (H2)*

Sell companies are expected to have higher rate of positive forecasts errors than buy companies. Therefore, the second hypothesis would be presented as:

H2: Sell companies have higher rate of positive forecasts errors than buy companies.

The study tests the proposed relationship of analysts' recommendations and forecasts errors by using the chi-square.

5.2.3.2.1 **Contingency Table**

In order to provide evidence that the analysts' recommendations do capture the incentive to conduct downward forecasts management to avoid negative forecasts errors, I examine the relation between: (1) the analysts' recommendations, and (2) the signs of forecasts errors (Meet). Table 5-7 presents contingency table.

Table 5-7. The contingency table that report the association between analysts' recommendations and positive forecasts errors for all of the companies.

Contingency table classifying firm-years based on (1) stock transaction status, and (2) sign of forecasts errors			
		forecasts errors	
		positive (Meet=1)	Negative (Meet =0)
Number of firm-years (% of firm years conditional on Buy or Sell	Sell	52.75% 1302	47.24% 1166
	Buy	49.13% 411	50.87% 406
Pearson Chi-square		$\chi2=1.36$ P=0.243	

The third and fourth columns summarize the relation between stock transaction status and forecasts errors (*MEET*). More than fifty per cent of the firm-quarters that are categorized as sell exceed management's expectations (*MEET* = 1), compared to 49.13 per cent of the firm-quarters categorized as buy. The Chi-square test indicates that the association is insignificant (χ^2= 1.36, p > 0.243). Table 5-7 indicates that there is no difference in the frequency of positive forecasts errors between buy and sell-companies. This shows that H2 is not supported.

5.2.3.2.2 **Analysis of Variance**

Next, in order to obtain better comparison of forecasts errors (H2) between buy and sell companies, the differences of means of forecasts errors between buy and sell companies are tested.

Table 5-8. Test of comparison of means of FE among companies that have been classified into the groups of buy and sell, according to their value of *AR* (for all of the companies)

	N (Mean) FE	Minimum (Maximum) FE	STDEV FE
Sell	2468 (-0.00021)	-0.008 (0.009)	0.003
Buy	817 (-0.0040)	-0.008 (0.007)	0.00294
All	3285 (0.00115)	-0.00885 (0.00974)	0.00298
Buy vs. sell	F 1.117	sig. 0.291	

In Table 5-8 the difference of measure of forecasts errors is not significant between the groups of buy and sell. The Table 5-8 indicates that, there is no significant difference in the forecasts errors of the buy and sell companies.

5.2.3.2.3 **Control Variables for testing the relationship of analysts' recommendations and forecasts errors**

Several control variables are included in testing the effect of AR on Forecasts errors. First, earnings management can affect forecast errors because managers can manipulate the reported earnings (McNichols 1989; Kasznik 1999) to create positive

203

forecasts errors. Kasznik (1999) discovered evidence that is consistent with managers issuing earnings forecast, and then manipulating earnings in order for it to fall aligned with the forecast. Thus, the firm's ability to influence earnings, as revealed by its discretionary accruals is incorporated as a control. A version of the cross-sectional modified Jones model is used to estimate discretionary accruals. Other control variables are the similar to those explained in the previous section (5.2.3.1.3).

To examine the relationship between the analysts' recommendations and forecasts errors, analogous to Matsumoto (2002), regression (4-14) is estimated (firm and time subscripts have been suppressed):

Results of the logit regression are indicated in Table 5-9.

Table 5-9. Logit Analysis of the probability of meeting or exceeding management forecasts

Model	$Prob(meet=1)= F(\alpha_0+\alpha_1\ AR+\alpha_2 FREQ+\alpha_3\ Difficulty + \alpha_4\ LMV+\alpha_5\ MB+\alpha_6 DA +\alpha_7 Hightech +\alpha_8 Lag\_loss + \alpha_9\ Year+\varepsilon)$			
Variable	**Predicted Sign**	**Coefficient**	**P-value**[b]	**Marginal Effect**
Intercept	?	-1.694	0.046	-
Incentive to avoid negative earnings surprises:				
AR	+	0.374	0.136	1.235
Control Variables				
Freq	-	-0.981	0. 002***	0.375
Difficulty	+	0.832	0.001***	8.879
LMV	+	0.147	0.344	1.159
MB	+	0.004	0.596	1.004
DA	+	0.000	0.590	1.000
Hightech	+	0.345	0.121	1.412
Lag_loss	+	0.555	0.077*	1.742
Year	-	0.571	0.015**	1.771

Log Likelihood	544.183	**Hosmer Lemeshow**	
Chi-square	170.837	Pearson Chi	4726.44
P-value	0.000	Prob	0.3028

a The dependent variable equals 1 if a firm's actual earnings meets or exceeds the managers' forecasts, 0 otherwise.

b. p-values are one-tailed.

*, **, *** P-values are significant at 10%, 5%, and 1% significance level.

In Table 5-9, columns 3 through 5 represent the results of the regression in the companies. The coefficient on *AR* is positive but insignificant, suggesting that sell stocks are unlikely to meet forecasts. The coefficient of *Freq* is negative and significant at 1%, consistent with Rogers and Stocken (2005), discovering that managers have fewer incentives to avoid negative surprises when the frequency of downward forecasts management from previous years is high. In addition, the coefficient on Difficulty is positive and significant, consistent with the Rogers and Stocken (2006) notion that managers have more incentives to avoid negative surprises when the recognition of forecasts management is more difficult for investors. Also consistent is the conjecture that those firms with low value-relevance of earnings have less incentive to avoid negative earnings surprises, while firms with lagged losses (*Lag_loss*) are more likely to meet or exceed their expectations. The positive but insignificant coefficient of *Hightech* implies that firms with relatively higher litigation prospects appear to be marginally more likely to avoid negative earnings surprises.

Column 5 reports the marginal effects of each variable. The marginal effects are similar to the slope's coefficients in an OLS regression (Kelly & Ljungqvist, 2012). The marginal effect for frequency is 0.375, suggesting that moving from the first to the third quartile of Freq decreases the probability of meeting, or exceeding analysts' expectations by approximately 62.5 per cent. The marginal effect for difficulty equals 8.879, indicating that an increase in the difficulty of predicting future profits increases the probability of meeting or exceeding the analysts' expectations by 780 per cent. The marginal effect for lag_loss is 0.742, indicating that in firms that reporting losses in the previous period, the probability of meeting or exceeding the analysts' expectations is lower by 26 per cent.

Thus, according to the logistic regression, there is no significant relationship between forecasts errors and analysts' recommendations (H2 is not supported).

5.2.3.3   *Comparing FM between the companies that have positive and negative forecasts errors (H3 and H4)*

It is expected that, the companies that meet forecasts are more likely to produce downward biased forecasts than the companies that do not meet forecasts. Therefore, the research hypothesis is stated as follows:

H3: In sell companies, companies that meet forecasts are more likely to do income decreasing FM than companies that do not meet forecasts.

In order to test the third hypothesis, the difference of mean forecasts management of the companies that possess positive FE, and the companies that possess negative FE in sell group are duly tested. The results of the test are shown in Table 5-10.

Table 5-10. Test of difference in mean forecasts management for the companies that meet managers' forecasts and the companies that miss forecasts in the sell (H3) companies.

		Sell	
	No.	Mean FM_Matsumoto	STDEV FM_Matsumoto
Positive or zero FE	1300	-0.0157	0.105
Negative FE	1165	-0.0042	0.12
		ANOVA's F	Sig.
		0.098	0.756

Testing the difference of the means of measure of forecasts management (*FM_Mutsomoto*) between companies that meet the forecasts, and the companies that miss forecasts in the group of Sell companies showed that there is no significant difference in the means of forecasts management between them. Therefore, the hypothesis H3 is not supported, which generally means that there is no significant difference in the means of forecasts management between the companies that meet or miss forecasts in the sell companies.

If the buy companies do not have downward forecasts management, then in the buy companies, companies that meet forecasts are not likely to do income decreasing FM to meet forecasts. Thus I expect the fourth hypothesis for the buy companies will note supported.

H4: There is no significant difference in income decreasing FM between buy companies that meet forecasts and those that do not meet forecasts.

In order to test the fourth hypotheses, the difference of mean forecasts management of the companies that possess positive FE, and the companies that possess negative FE in buy group is duly tested. The results of the test are shown in Table 5-11.

Table 5-11. Test of difference in mean forecasts management for the companies that meet managers' forecasts and the companies that miss forecasts in the buy (H4) companies.

		Buy	
	No.	Mean FM_Matsumoto	STDEV FM_Matsumoto
Positive or zero FE	408	-0.0032	0.0968
Negative FE	401	-0.00195	0.1128
		ANOVA's F	Sig.
		1.222	0.274
*, **: Significance at 0.1 and 0.05			

Testing the difference of the means of measure of forecasts management (*FM_Mutsomoto*) between companies that meet the forecasts, and the companies that miss forecasts in the groups of Buy companies showed that there is no significant difference in the means of forecasts management between them. Therefore, the hypothesis H4 is supported, which generally means that there is no significant difference in the means of forecasts management between the companies that meet or miss forecasts in the buy companies.

5.2.3.4 *Test of difference in positive forecasts errors using unmanaged and issued forecasts (H5 and H6)*

In order to see whether sell companies produce downward biased forecasts to achieve positive forecasts errors, the fifth hypothesis was formulated.

H5: For sell companies, incidence of positive forecasts errors will decrease when forecasts errors are based on "unmanaged" rather than issued forecasts.

Table 5-12 reflect the frequency of positive forecasts errors when forecasts errors are calculated using unmanaged and issued forecasts. Table 5-12 focuses only on the forecasts errors of the sell-companies.

Table 5-12. Comparison of the frequency of positive
forecasts errors between forecasts errors that are
calculated using unmanaged and issued forecasts in the
sell companies (first subsample)

		proxies for forecasts management FM_Matsumoto	
		Positive	Negative
Number of firm-years (% of firm years) conditional on FE with "Unmanaged" and issued forecasts	FE with "Unmanaged" forecasts	50.58% 1246	49.42% 1217
	FE with issued forecasts	52.72% 1300	47.27% 1165
	Pearson Chi-square	$\chi2 = 2.28$ $P = 0.131$	

As indicated by Table 5-12, the frequency of forecasts errors that
are calculated using unbiased forecasts are lower than the
frequencies of positive forecasts errors that are calculated by using
issued forecasts. However the significance of the difference
between the frequencies of positive forecasts errors is not as strong.
Thus, Table 5-12 only represents weak evidence that supports the
fact that in sell companies' negative forecasts management
causes the positive forecasts errors. This finding however, weakly
supports H5.

To see whether in buy companies, the negative forecasts
management is conducted to achieve positive forecasts errors the
sixth hypothesis was formulated.

H6: For buy companies, the frequency of positive forecasts errors is not expected to decrease when forecasts errors are based on "unmanaged" rather than issued forecasts.

As a result of running the same frequency test in the buy companies, Table 5-13 reflects the frequencies of positive forecasts errors when the forecasts errors are calculated by using unmanaged and issued forecasts. Incidentally, Table 5-13 only focuses on the buy companies.

Table 5-13. Comparison of the frequency of positive forecasts errors between forecasts errors that are calculated using unmanaged and issued forecasts in the buy companies (first subsample)

| | | proxies for forecasts management FM_Matsumoto | |
		Positive	negative
Number of firm-years (% of firm years) conditional on FE with "Unmanaged" and issued forecasts	FE with "Unmanaged" forecasts	44.76% 370	55.23% 439
	FE with issued forecasts	50.43% 408	49.56% 401
	Pearson Chi-square	$\chi 2 = 3.49$ P = 0.06	

As indicated by Table 5-13, the frequency of positive forecasts errors when using issued forecast is not (significantly) higher than the frequency of forecasts errors issued by unbiased forecasts. Therefore, in contrast to the sell companies, when the buy companies do forecasts management, they will not have higher positive forecast errors compared to when there is no forecasts management. Thus, H6 is supported.

Therefore, although the negative forecast management in sell companies is higher than the negative forecasts management in the buy companies, based on the sample of all companies, I discovered weak evidence that among the buy and sell companies, the companies issue negative forecasts management to achieve positive forecasts errors.

As previously stated, it is expected that firms that just meet the expectations are more likely to conduct forecast management compared to firms that just fail to meet expectations, along with the firms that just beat the expectations. However, based on the sample of all of the companies, the findings failed to support this argument. Moreover, based on Burgestahler and Eams (2006) and Matsumoto (2003) allegations, it is expected that the negative forecasts management occur in the companies that possess small forecasts errors. Keeping such an expectation in mind, the next section tests the hypotheses by taking into account the companies that are within the small distance around zero forecasts errors.

5.2.4   Analysis for the Companies with Small Positive or Negative Forecasts Errors

Burgstahler and Eames (2006) and Abarbanell and Lehavy (2003b) argued that the benefit of forecast management to a firm is the increase of the amount of forecast management, however, forecast management also imposes an unduly cost on the firm. If there is a sudden drop in the marginal benefit at the point just to the right of the zero surprise point for many firms, then zero surprise is the optimal level a firm should achieve by conducting forecast management. Realistically, there might indeed be a sudden drop in the marginal benefit for many firms. The benefit to the firms just meeting expectations is much larger than that for firms that fail to meet the expectations by a small margin, whereas the benefit to firms that beat the expectations is only marginally larger than the benefit to firms that just meet expectations. This argument implies that firms that just meet the expectations are more likely to conduct forecast management compared to firms that just fail to meet expectations and firms that beat expectations.

Based on Burgstahler and Eames (2002) positions, the hypotheses will be retested only by accounting for the companies that are in a small distance around zero forecasts errors. The distance of a 0.5 standard deviation of forecasts errors on the left and right side of zero forecast error is taken as small distance around the zero forecasts error. The distance of 0.5 standard deviation is chosen due to the fact that it is small and also a considerable number of companies exist in this sphere.

5.2.4.1 *Relationship of Analysts Recommendation and Forecasts Management (H1)*

Sell companies are expected to have more pessimistic (less optimistic) forecasts management. Therefore, the research hypothesis is presented as follows:

H1: Sell companies issue more pessimistic forecasts than buy companies.

The study tests the proposed relationship of analysts' recommendations and forecasts management by using the chi-square test.

5.2.4.1.1 **Contingency table**

Similar to section 5.2.3, chi-square tests have been used to test for the difference in the frequency of negative forecasts management in the buy side and sell side companies. The following contingency table (Table 5-14) shows the result of the test of difference in incidence of negative forecasts management in buy and sell companies.

Table 5-14. Association between analysts'
recommendations and downward forecasts
managements for the companies that have
near zero forecasts errors.

		proxies for forecasts management FM_Matsumoto	
Contingency table classifying firm-years based on (1) analysts' recommendations, and (2) sign of forecasts managements			
		Positive	Negative
Number of firm-years (% of firm years conditional on Buy or Sell	Sell	28.12% 253	71.87% 646
	Buy	36.72% 112	63.27% 193
Pearson Chi-square		$\chi2$ = 6.74 P= 0009	

As Table 5-14 indicates, sell companies have a
significantly higher incidence of negative $FM\_Matsumoto$
compared to buy companies.

5.2.4.1.2 Analysis of Variance

To see whether there is a significant difference between the
buy and sell companies in their practice of conducting forecasts
management, the difference in the mean of the forecasts
management between the buy and sell companies was tested.

Table 5-15 shows the comparison results of the means of forecasts
management measure ($FM\_Matsumoto$) between buy and sell
companies.

Table 5-15. Test of comparison of means *FM* among companies that have been classified into the groups of buy and sell, according to their value of *AR* (for the companies that have near zero forecasts errors)

	N (Mean)	Minimum (Maximum)	STDEV
	FM_Matsumoto	FM_Matsumoto	
Sell	899 (-0.00244)	-0.00250 (0.00312)	0.00085
Buy	305 (0.000257)	-0.00029 (0.00472)	0.00075
All	1204 (-0.00194)	-0.00250 (0.00472)	0.00079
Buy vs. sell	F 8.900	sig. 0.003**	

As Table 5-15indicates, there is a significant difference between the mean of forecasts management between buy and sell, considering, $FM\_Matsumoto$. The sign of differences with regards to $FM\_Matsumoto$ measure confirms the first hypothesis, due to the fact that there is a lower mean for forecasts management for sell companies than for buy companies.

5.2.4.1.3 Control Variables for Testing the Relationship of Analysts' Recommendations and Forecasts Management

Including the control variables in the relationship between analysts' recommendations and forecasts management logistic regression has been used. In the logistic regression forecasts management, measures are used as dependent variables and the analysts' recommendations act as independent variables. Table 5-16 shows the result of the logistic regression.

Table 5-16. The results of logistic regression for the second subsample.

Model	$Prob(Down=1)=F(a_0+a_1AR+a_2AR \times Difficulty+a_3AR \times FREQ+a_4LMV+a_5MB+a_6$ $Hightech +a \cdot Log\_Loss+a_7Year)$					
Dependent Variable: down=1 if ???? ?? ???????? is negative and down=0 otherwise						
Variable Dependents	Predicted sign	Coefficients FM (Matsumoto)		p-values FM (Matsumoto)		Marginal effects FM (Matsumoto)
Independents:						
Constant	?	-1.750		0.892		-
AR	+	0.699		0.000***		2.012
Moderating Variables:						
AR×Difficulty	-	2.662		0.021**		14.323
AR×Freq	-	-0.151		0.019**		0.860
Control Variables:						
LMV	+	0.353		0.023**		1.424
MB	-	-0.003		0.686		0.995
Hightech	+	-0.181		0.102		0.834
Log_Loss	+	+0.739		0.098*		1.538
Year	-	-1.223		0.000***		0.294
Log Likelihood		564.435	Hosmer Lemeshow			
Chi-square		59.383	Pearson Chi	510.13		
P-value		0.000	Prob	0.246		

*, **,*** Significant at 0.1, 0.05 and 0.01 levels, respectively based on one-tailed tests for signed predictions, two-tailed tests otherwise.

According to Table 5-16, the coefficients of AR are positive. This indicates that when the AR for the company is high (i.e. the company is in sell position), the companies produce more downward biased forecasts than when the AR is low (the company

218

is in buy position). On the other hand, the coefficient of $AR \times Freq$ is significantly negative. This shows that frequency of previous year's forecasts management plays a moderating role in the relationship of AR and forecasts management. The coefficient of $AR \times Difficulty$ is significantly positive, indicating that when it is more difficult for analysts and investors to forecast the company's profit, the company will produce more downward biased forecasts.

The marginal effects are analogous to the slope coefficients in an OLS regression (Kelly & Ljungqvist, 2012). The marginal effect for AR is 2.012, suggesting that moving from the first to the third quartile of AR causes the probability of meeting or exceeding the expectations increases by approximately 101 per cent.

The coefficient of $AR \times Difficulty$ is positive and significant, indicating that it is more difficult for investors to recognize the credibility of the managers' forecasts, the more management will produce downward biased forecasts. It is important to remember that according to the factor analysis in section 4.3.2.3, the values for difficulty ranges from -0.58 to 0.84, where the lower values for this variable represent a lesser difficulty, while a higher value represents a higher difficulty. Since the scale for the difficulty is relatively small, it might not be surprising to have greater numbers for the marginal effect of difficulties. The value of the marginal effects of $AR \times$

Difficulty is 14.323, showing that the most for the most difficult firm, the probability of forecasts management is approximately 1ᴇ.3 times compared to the least difficult firms. Also, the coefficients of LMV, MB and lag_loss are significant, and contain their expected values.

5.2.4.2 *Relationship of Analysts' recommendations and Forecasts Errors (H2)*

Sell companies are expected to have higher rate of positive forecasts errors than buy companies. Therefore, the second hypothesis would be presented as:

H2: Sell companies have higher rate of positive forecasts errors than buy companies.

The study tests the proposed relationship of analysts' recommendations and forecasts errors by using the chi-square test.

5.2.4.2.1 **Contingency Table**

In order to provide evidence that the analysts' recommendations do capture the incentive to conduct downward forecasts management to avoid negative forecasts errors, I examine the relation between: (1) the analysts' recommendations, and (2) the signs of forecasts errors (Meet)). Table 5-17presents contingency test.

Table 5-17. Association between analysts'
recommendations and positive forecasts
errors for the companies that have near
zero forecasts errors.

		forecasts errors	
Contingency table classifying firm-years based on (1) analysts' recommendations, and (2) sign of forecasts errors			
		Positive	Negative
Number of firm-years (% of firm years conditional on Buy or Sell	Sell	53.06% 480	46.96% 424
	Buy	59.22% 184	40.78% 123
Pearson Chi-square		$\chi^2 = 4.28$ P=0.038	

As Table 5-17 indicates, sell companies have a significantly less incidence of positive forecasts errors than the buy companies.

5.2.4.2.2 Analysis of Variance

To see whether there is a significant difference between the buy and sell companies in their practice of conducting forecasts management to meet forecasts, the difference in the mean of the forecasts errors between the buy and sell companies was tested. It is expected that the reason that the sell companies do more downward forecasts management compared to buy companies is to meet their respective forecasts.

Table 5-18shows the comparison results of the means of forecasts errors between buy and sell companies.

221

Table 5-18. Test of comparison of means *FE* among companies that have been classified into the groups of Buy and sell, according to their value of ***AR*** (for the companies that have near zero forecasts errors)

	N (Mean)	Minimum (Maximum)	STDEV
	FE	*FE*	*FE*
Sell	904 (0.000111)	-0.0084 (0.0092)	0.0003
Buy	307 (0.0000784)	-0.0085 (0.0068)	0.00029
All	1211 (0.000106)	-0.00854 (0.00923)	0.0003
	F	**sig.**	
Buy vs. sell	1.121	0.291	

As Table 5-18indicates, there is not a significant difference between the mean of forecasts errors between buy and sell. Therefore the second hypothesis was not supported

5.2.4.2.3 Control Variables for testing the relationship of analysts' recommendations and forecasts errors

For testing the relationship of AR and FE by including control variables in small distance around zero forecasts errors, the logit regression of the probability of meeting or exceeding the forecasts against the *AR* was ran. The results of the logit regression are shown in Table 5-19.

Table 5-19. Logit Analysis of the probability of meeting or exceeding managers' forecasts and the incentives to avoid negative earnings surprises for the second subsample.

Model		$Prob(meet=1)= F(\alpha_0+\alpha_1\,AR+\alpha_2\,Freq+\alpha_3\,Difficulty + \alpha_4\,LMV+\alpha_5\,MB+\alpha_6Hightech +\alpha_7Lag\_loss+\alpha_8\,Year+\varepsilon)$		
Variable	Predicted Sign	Coefficient	P-value[b]	Marginal Effect
Intercept	?	-1.217	0.198	-
Incentive to avoid negative earnings surprises:				
AR	+	-0.381	0.032	0.464
Control Variables				
Freq	-	-0.890	0.002***	0.411
Difficulty	+	0.960	0.001***	2.117
LMV	+	0.200	0.355	1.221
M/B	+	0.003	0.540	1.003
DA	+	0.021	0.816	0.899
High-tech	+	0.288	0.117	1.334
Lag_loss	-	-0.573	0.028**	0.459
Year	-	0.561	0.016**	1.762
Log Likelihood		544.018	**Hosmer Lemeshow**	
Chi-square		171.032	Pearson Chi	639.78
P-value		0.000	Prob	0.6263
No. of observations				
Meet/Exceed		740		
Did not meet		563		
Total		1303		

*, **,*** Significant at 0.1, 0.05 and 0.01 levels
a. The dependent variable equals 1 if a firm's actual earnings meets or exceeds the managers' forecasts, 0 otherwise.
b. p-values are one-tailed.

Contradicting the expectations, in small distances around zero forecasts error, sell companies do not have higher positive forecasts errors. The positive coefficient of $Difficulty$ indicates that the more difficult it is for the market to predict a company's profit, the more the company will experience positive forecasts errors. The negative coefficient of frequency is consistent with Rogers and Stocken (2005), indicating that when the company contain a high frequency of downward biased forecasts in the previous years, the probability of having positive forecasts errors decreases in the current year.

The coefficient of lag_loss is negative and significant, indicating that the companies that have lagged loss have lower positive forecasts errors. In addition, the coefficient of $Year$ is positive and significant, indicating that in 2010, the companies have higher positive forecasts errors compared to the previous year.

5.2.4.3 *Comparing FM between the companies that have positive and negative forecasts errors (H3 and H4)*

It is expected that, the companies that meet forecasts are more likely to produce downward biased forecasts than the companies that do not meet forecasts. Therefore, the research hypothesis is stated as follows:

H3: In sell companies, companies that meet forecasts are more likely to do income decreasing FM than companies that do not meet forecasts.

In order to test for H3 and H4 again by using the companies that have small forecasts errors, the analysis of the variance is utilized to test the difference in the means of forecasts management between the companies that possesses positive and negative forecasts errors. Table 5-20 presents the results of the tests of the means of forecasts management between the companies that meet the forecasts, and companies that do not meet forecasts in the buy and the sell groups (H3 and H4). The test is conducted on the companies in the subsample near zero forecasts errors.

Table 5-20. Test of significance of
difference in mean FM for the
companies that meet the forecasts and
the companies that miss the forecast in
the sell groups for the companies that
have near zero forecasts errors.

		Sell	
	No.	Mean *FM_Matsumoto*	STDEV *FM_Matsumoto*
Positive or zero FE	467	-0.00499	0.0080
Negative FE	432	0.00068	0.0115
		ANOVA"s F	Sig.
		5.1830	0.023**

*, **: Significance at 0.1 and 0.05 respectively.

Table 5-20showed that when focusing on the companies
that are within small distance around zero forecast error, there is a
significant difference in the means of FM for companies that meet
forecasts, and companies that miss forecasts in sell groups (H3
supported). In group of sell companies, the companies that meet
forecasts have lower mean forecasts management than the
companies that miss forecasts.

If the buy companies do not have downward forecasts management, then in the buy companies, companies that meet forecasts are not likely to do income decreasing FM to meet forecasts. It is expected that the fourth hypothesis for the buy companies will not be supported.

H4: There is no significant difference in income decreasing FM between buy companies that meet forecasts and those that do not meet forecasts.

In order to test for H4 again by using the companies that have small forecasts errors, the analysis of the variance is utilized to test the difference in the means of forecasts management between the companies that possesses positive and negative forecasts errors. Table 5-21 presents the results of the tests of the means of forecasts management between the companies that meet the forecasts, and companies that do not meet forecasts in the buy group (H4). The test is conducted on the companies in the subsample near zero forecasts errors.

Table 5-21. Test of significance of difference in mean FM for the companies that meet the forecasts and the companies that miss the forecast in the buy group for the companies that have near zero forecasts errors.

	Buy		
	No.	Mean FM_Matsumoto	STDEV FM_Matsumoto
Positive or zero FE	180	-0.00499	0.00958
Negative FE	125	0.00246	0.01038
		ANOVA"s F	Sig.
		2.7457	0.098*

*, **: Significance at 0.1 and 0.05 respectively.

Table 5-21showed that, in group of buy companies, the companies that meet forecasts have lower mean forecasts management than the companies that miss forecasts. However, the difference of FM for companies that meet forecasts and companies that miss forecasts in the buy group is not significant at a 0.05 significance level (H4 is supported).

5.2.4.4 *Test of difference in the frequency of positive forecasts errors using unmanaged and issued forecasts (H5 and H6)*

In order to see whether sell companies do downward forecasts management to achieve positive forecasts errors, the fifth hypothesis was formulated.

H5: For sell companies, incidence of positive forecasts errors will decrease when forecasts errors are based on "unmanaged" rather than issued forecasts.

The Chi-square tests have been utilized to compare the differences in the frequency of positive forecasts errors using unmanaged and issued forecasts. Table 5-22 reflects the frequency of positive forecasts errors when the forecasts errors are calculated using unmanaged and issued forecasts. The table only use the forecasts errors of the sell companies that have small forecasts errors.

Table 5-22. Comparison of the frequency of
positive forecasts errors between forecasts errors
that are calculated using "unmanaged" and
issued forecasts. For the sell companies that
have near zero FE

		proxies for forecasts management	
		FM_Matsumoto	
		Positive	negative
Number of firm-years (% of firm years conditional on FE with "Unmanaged" and issued forecasts	FE with "Unmanaged" forecasts	43.03% 387	56.95% 511
	FE with issued forecasts	51.94% 467	48.05% 432
	Pearson Chi-square	$\chi 2 = 13.92$ $P = 0.0001$	

As indicated by Table 5-22, the frequency of positive forecasts errors that are calculated using unbiased forecasts is lower than the frequency of positive forecasts errors that are calculated using issued forecasts. Thus, it is obvious that on the sell companies, the negative forecasts management caused the positive forecasts errors. Thus, H5 is duly supported.

To see whether in buy companies, the negative forecasts management is conducted to achieve positive forecasts errors the sixth hypothesis was formulated.

H6: For buy companies, the frequency of positive forecasts errors is not expected to decrease when forecasts errors are based on "unmanaged" rather than issued forecasts.

Table 5-23 reflects the frequencies of positive forecasts errors when forecasts managements are calculated using unmanaged and issued forecasts. Table 5-23 only focuses on the buy companies that have small forecasts errors.

Table 5-23. Comparison of the frequency of positive forecasts errors between forecasts errors that are calculated using unmanaged and issued forecasts for the buy companies that have near zero FE

		proxies for forecasts management	
		FM_Matsumoto	
		Positive	negative
Number of firm-years (% of firm years conditional on FE with "Unmanaged" and issued forecasts	FE with "Unmanaged" forecasts	51.11% 156	48.85% 149
	FE with issued forecasts	59.01% 180	40.98% 125
	Pearson Chi-square	$\chi2 = 3.35$	
		$P = 0.067$	

As indicated by Table 5-23, the frequency of positive forecasts errors with issued forecast is not significantly higher than the frequency of positive forecasts errors by unbiased forecasts. Therefore, contradicting what has been observed so far for sell companies, in the buy companies, when the companies conduct forecasts management, they will not obtain higher positive forecast errors compared to when there is no forecasts management. Thus, H6 is supported.

231

5.2.5 Summary of the Findings

To summarise the findings in accordance to the frequency table and ANOVA in Table 5-14 and Table 5-15, it is discovered that negative forecasts managements in sell companies are higher than the negative forecasts managements in buy companies. However, there is no difference in the incidences and means of positive forecasts errors between the buy and sell companies. In addition, the logistic regressions of Table 5-16 shows that, sell companies produce more downward biased forecasts compared to buy companies. Tests of the difference in means of forecasts management between the companies that meet or do not meet their forecasts shows that in sell companies, the companies that meet forecasts have higher negative forecasts managements compared to the companies that miss forecasts. However, this result does not apply for the buy companies. In addition, as a result of testing whether the negative forecasts management in the sell companies lead to positive forecasts errors, the test of frequency (Table 5-22) shows that in the sell companies, the negative forecasts management directly result in a positive forecast error. However, in the buy side companies, the negative forecast management does not lead to positive forecasts errors. Therefore, the findings can be summarised as in the sell (buy) companies the companies do (not do) negative forecasts management to achieve positive forecasts errors. **Error! Reference source not found.** summarizes the f indings.

Table **Error! No text of specified style in document.**-1. Summary of the findings

	All companies			Small distance around zero FE		
Tables	Chi-square	Analysis of variance	Logistic regression	Chi-square	Analysis of variance	Logistic regression
H1	S	N	S	S	S	S
H2	N	N	N	N	N	N
H3		N			S	
H4		S			S	
H5	N			S		
H6	S			S		

S= Supported , N= Not supported

For the companies that are in small distance around zero forecast errors, all of the tests support H1. When considering all of the companies only in case of analysis of variance do not support H1. Therefore, since in the subsample near zero forecasts errors, all of the tests support H1, and for all of the companies, 2 out of 3 tests support H1, and the overall findings firmly support H1.

None of the tests in any of the samples support H2, which makes H2 untenable. This means that sell companies do not possess higher positive forecasts errors. The reason might be that buy companies might have used income increasing earnings management strategy to meet the forecasts. In order to produce positive forecasts errors, the income increasing earnings management in buy companies might have been more efficient than income decreasing FMs in sell companies.

233

With regards to H3, while the findings of analysis of variance support H3 in small distance around zero forecasts errors, when all companies are considered, there is no support for H3. Therefore, only considering the small distance around zero forecasts errors, H3 is supported. This means that in sell companies of subsample 2, the companies that meet or beat forecasts possess more downward FM than companies that fail to meet their forecasts. Thus, in this subsample, H3 is supported.

Regarding the findings of Analysis of Variance, there is support for H4 in small distance around zero FE. Additionally, H4 is supported for all of the companies. Therefore, the findings support H4.

The chi-square test supports H5 in a subsample of companies that have near zero forecasts errors. However, when all of the companies are taken into the chi-square test does not support H5. Thus, considering the subsample near zero forecast errors, H5 is staunchly supported. This shows that, in the sell companies, the negative forecasts management caused the positive forecasts errors.

The chi-square test support H6 in the subsample of all the companies, and the companies that have near zero forecasts errors. So, H6 is supported.

The findings show that while sell companies produce more downward biased forecasts, and such downward biased forecasts lead to positive forecasts errors. However, sell companies do not have higher positive forecasts errors compared to buy companies.

Overall, the results reveal that while H1, H3, H4, H5 and H6 are supported, H2is not supported. The next chapter interpret these findings in detail.

Chapter 6. CONCLUSION AND DISCUSSION

6.1   Introduction

As mentioned earlier in Chapter 1 (introduction) and Chapter 2 (review of literature), this research is about the effect of analysts' recommendations, in terms of buy (growth companies) and sell (non-growth companies) recommendations, on forecasts management. Keeping in line with this theme, Chapter 3 viewed the methods of the study and the tests that were ran on two subsamples of all the companies, and the companies that are in small distance near zero forecasts errors.

The first part of Chapter 4 reported the statistical results based on all of the companies. The findings from the first part showed a significant, but weak relationship between the analysts' recommendations and forecasts management. In other word, when all of the companies are considered, sell companies reported significantly higher pessimistic forecasts compared to their buy counterparts (H1 supported).However, such negative forecasts management does not create higher positive forecasts errors (H3 and H5 supported). Similarly, in the buy companies, the negative forecasts management does not lead to positive forecasts errors (H4 and H6 are supported). In addition, there is no significant difference in the frequency of positive forecasts errors in the buy and the sell companies (H2 not supported).

236

Consistent with the notion that companies that just meet forecasts are more likely to conduct forecast management than companies that just fail to meet forecasts and firms that beat forecasts (Burgstahler and Eams 2006, Abarbanell and Lehavy 2003b), the second part of Chapter 4 has been dedicated to the statistical findings based on the companies that are in small distance near zero forecasts errors. The findings discussed in the second part shows that sell companies have higher pessimistic forecasts than buy companies (H1 supported). In addition, in the sell [buy] companies group, the companies that have positive forecasts errors [do not] issue higher pessimistic forecasts (H3 and H4 supported). Such pessimistic forecasts [do not] lead to higher positive forecasts errors (H5 and H6 supported). However, the ration of positive forecasts errors does not differ between the buy and sell companies (H2 not supported).

This chapter summarizes the results and findings discussed in the preceding chapter. It also contains recommendations for future studies, and highlights the practical and theoretical implications of the findings for policy makers, along with investors. This will be followed by a description of the limitations of the research. The chapter finishes with a brief conclusion of the study.

6.2 Discussion: Overview of the Findings

Back to the research objective in chapter one, the main objective of this research is to examine the effects of analysts' recommendations representing the growth and non-growth companies on the managers' decisions towards forecasts management. The main objective was divided into the following three sub objectives:

6.2.1 Research Objective 1: To examine whether *sell companies* tend to actively engage in producing downward biased forecasts compared to *buy companies.*

To achieve this objective, in the previous chapter, the effect of the analysts' recommendations on forecasts management was shown by regressing forecasts management on analysts' recommendations. Additional tests on the relationship of analysts' recommendations, and forecasts management were conducted by dividing the companies into groups of buy and sell, according to the analysts' recommendations, and examining the ratio of positive to negative forecast errors in buy and sell companies. It was shown that, although in general there is weak difference between the buy and sell companies in terms of downward forecasts management, in the companies that are within small distance around zero forecasts errors, there is higher frequency of downward forecasts management in the sell companies compared to the buy companies.

6.2.2 Research Objective 2: To examine whether *sell companies* are more likely to achieve positive forecasts errors than *buy companies.*

To achieve this objective, the effect of analysts' recommendation on forecasts errors was shown by regressing forecasts errors on analysts' recommendations. Additional tests on the relationship of analysts' recommendations and forecasts errors were conducted by dividing companies into groups of buy and sell according to the analysts' recommendations, and examining the ratio of positive to negative forecasts errors in buy and sell companies. It was shown that, there is not higher frequency of positive forecast errors in sell companies compared to buy companies.

6.2.3 Research Objective 3: To examine the effect of the analysts' recommendations on management's decisions in producing downward biased forecast to reach positive forecasts errors.

In addition, based on the test result of the relationship of the forecasts management and forecasts errors for the companies that possess small forecasts errors, it was determined that in the sell companies group, companies having positive forecasts errors have higher means of negative forecasts management. However, such results are inapplicable for buy companies. This finding implies that sell companies conduct negative forecasts management to realize positive forecasts errors. Moreover, in the sell group, the frequency of positive forecasts errors that are calculated using "unmanaged" forecasts is significantly lower than the frequency of positive forecasts errors that are calculated by using reported forecasts. This provides additional evidence, and confirms that sell companies produce more downward biased forecasts just in order to avoid negative forecasts errors.

6.3   The Moderating Effect

6.3.1   Frequency

Studies have examined the effect of prior managers' forecast accuracy on investor expectations (Hirst et al. 1999) and managers' forecast as warnings in the face of earnings surprise (Kaznik and Lev 1995). Hirst et al. (1999) provide evidence that investor expectations are influenced by prior management's forecast accuracy interacting with the forecast form.

Following the previous findings stipulating that the market does learn from a company's history of forecast management, it is found that companies adjust their forecast management behaviours to be consistent with the learning effect. Although forecasts management can be predicted via the analysts' recommendations, the accuracy of the predictability is reduced in tandem with a company managing its forecasts downward during the previous years. Moreover, because of market learning, the more the companies managed their forecasts downward in the previous periods, the less able will be in meeting forecasts in the current period.

The findings in this research is consistent with Park and Stice (2000) who show that investor beliefs about the usefulness of a forecast are a function of both the accuracy and length of the prior forecasting record. Hutton and Stocken (2009) adopt Chen et al.'s (2005) Bayesian model to apply to investors' learning of managers' forecast accuracy. They realize that the stock price reaction to managers' forecast news is rising in prior forecast precision and also in the size of a company's forecasting record.

6.3.2 Difficulty

Managers make both good and bad news forecasts. Studies have shown that the difficulty in assessing the credibility of managers' disclosures may induce bias involuntary disclosures (Hui, 2012). For example, Penman (1980) and Lev & Penman (1990) reveal that, managers are aware of how they are observed by investors and analysts and the effect of forecasts on their status. Dambara (2012) state that, as the difficulty of verifiability rises, managers' misrepresentation turn out to be harder to notice with any degree of confidence, thereby rising the bias in forecasts (Dambra, Wasley, & Wu, 2012).

In addition, Rogers and Stocken (2005) obtained evidence to propose that management's motivation to release biased forecasts tends to be subject on the complexity for investors to perceive the bias. The findings of this research are consistent with the notion of Rogers and Stocken (2005), Hui (2012) and Dambra (2012) that present that managers are more expected to bias their earnings forecasts in circumstances where the market has greater complexity identifying distortion (Rogers, Van Buskirk, & Zechman, 2011). In fact, the findings show that when the recognition of biased forecasts by investors is difficult, the relationship between analysts' recommendations and forecasts management will be strengthened. In other words, sell companies do more downward forecasts management to realize positive forecasts errors.

In addition, the findings are consistent with the notion of Hui (2012), Cheng (2013) and Xu (2009) in showing that, difficult companies are more likely to achieve positive forecasts errors.

Similar to Cheng (2013) this study believes that managers are more expected to strategically choose forecast precision when investors have greater difficulty in evaluating the precision of their information.

To summarize, it is assumed that the investors will react more strongly to the forecasts issued by managers when the investors have greater difficulty assessing the business (Yang, 2012), which will consequently affect the bias in the managers' forecasts.

6.4 Implications of the Findings

The main result of this study is that the strategy that the companies undertake in order to avoid just missing the forecasts is strongly related to the recommendation position of the companies, which purports that market status generates serious incentives for management to conduct forecast management that creates positive forecast errors. One likely reason for such findings is that sell companies manage forecasts downward in order to be able to meet or beat their respective forecasts. By beating forecasts, they can generate positive forecasts errors (Brown, 2001; Matsumoto, 2002; and Burgstahler and Eames, 2006), or avoid the negative consequences of missing forecasts (Baginski & Hassell, 1990; Dye, 1983; Pinello, 2004). Such behaviour of sell companies can be explained by the prospect theory, which was explained in chapter 2.

Furthermore, there is a significant difference in the mean of forecasts management between the companies that possesses positive and negative forecasts errors in sell groups. However, this difference is <u>less</u> significant for the companies that are on the buy group. This implies that sell companies issue pessimistic forecasts to produce positive forecasts errors. Such implication is strengthened by further findings, which indicates that when forecasts managements are removed from managers' forecasts, there is a significant decrease in the rate of occurrences of positive forecasts errors for the sell companies (H5 supported), whereas the frequency of positive forecasts errors is not significantly affected for buy companies (H6 is supported). That is without negative forecasts management sell companies, are incapable of producing positive forecasts errors. In other words, the negative forecasts management in the sell companies is merely done to produce positive forecasts errors. This finding complements the result of Abarbanell and Lehavy (2003b), which suggests that instead of producing downward biased forecasts, buy companies engage in income increasing earnings management to meet or beat the analysts' forecasts. This study discovered that sell companies engage more in producing downward biased forecasts to create meetable or beatable forecasts. The reason might be that by having positive forecasts errors, first, the management of sell companies are more likely to manage the stock market expectations; and second, the management of sell companies are more likely to avoid the unfavourable and utility minimizing consequences that usually occur after missing forecasts such as the loss of reputation, litigation or takeovers. The findings, which fit in the framework, are summarized in

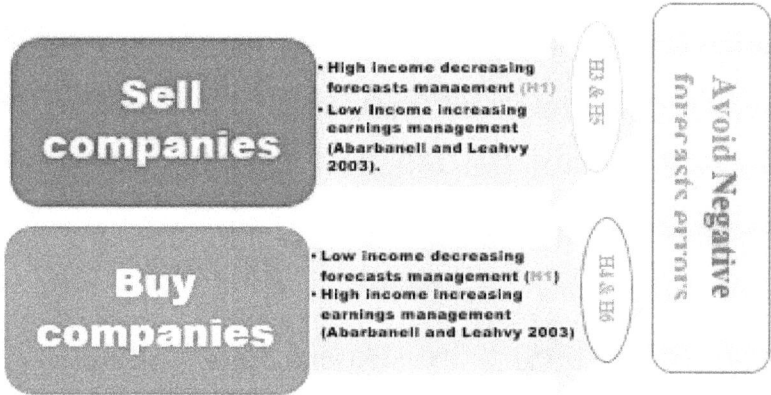

Figure 6-1.

Figure 6-1. Summary of the results of the hypotheses.

Previous researchers discovered that the management uses downward biased forecasts to produce positive earnings surprises

(Kasznik, 1999b). However, it was unclear whether their result would be valid in the presence of different analysts' recommendations. This study investigated the effect of analysts' recommendations on the management's decision to conduct FM to assess the extent at which the analysts' recommendations affect the managers' decisions to conduct FM to produce positive FEs.

6.5 Review of Framework and Contribution of Findings

Studying the determinants of managers' forecast precision is imperative. The reason is that a better understanding of the factors affecting management's choice of forecast precision can provide investors and other users with clues regarding the characteristics of the information contained in the forecasts. In addition, as the regulators assess the regulation of voluntary management disclosures, they need to better understand how managers select forecast precision disclosure alternatives (Hsu, 2011).

This research adds to the literature by searching for an additional factor that affects management decisions toward issuing forecasts. It has been found that the companies' growth status that is represented by the analysts' recommendations influences the management's decision to conduct forecasts management. This is supported by the finding that sell companies do downward forecasts management to realize positive forecasts errors (H3 and

H5 supported), whereas buy companies do not (H4 and H6 are supported).

Following the framework that was developed by Dutta and Gigler (2006), where the provision of forecast prevent the manager from managing earnings, which renders the earnings forecasts to assist in the process of transparent financial reporting, this research investigated the hypothesized effects of the analysts' recommendations on forecast management. This is consistent with the framework of Dutta and Gigler (2006), while Abarbanell and Lehavy (2003b) shows that buy companies do income increasing earnings management to avoid negative forecasts errors, sell companies produce more downward biased forecasts to avoid negative forecasts errors, and its consequent market punishments that unfavourably affects the management's utility.

The next two sections explain the behaviour of buy and sell companies.

6.5.1 Behavior of the Buy Companies

Burgstahler & Eames (2002) provided an insight into why forecast management is more evident for sell firms than it is for buy firms. They argued that, since there may be incremental benefits to beating rather than just meeting the forecasts, such benefit to a firm should increase the amount of forecast management. However, forecast management also imposes an unavoidable cost on the firm. The reason why sell companies do downward forecasts management to reach positive earnings surprise is that, the cost of negative forecasts management for sell firms is less than the cost of negative forecasts management for buy firms. Since stock price of the sell firms are less susceptible to earnings news (Abarbnell and Lehavy 2003b), the downward forecasts management of sell firms have less undesirable consequences on stock price than the downward forecasts management of the buy firms. On the other hand, the downward forecasts management of the sell firms help them to prevent experiencing the negative consequences of missing the forecasts which comes in the form of litigation, takeover, or contract termination (Beniluz, 2007; Frost, 1997; Kim & Shi, 2011). Therefore, the negative forecasts management of sell firms should be higher than the negative forecasts management for buy firms.

Furthermore, since the buy firms possess favourable forecasting records, investors are more responsive to their forecasted news, such firms would like to have their private information more fully impounded into their stock prices, and consequently, are more capable of reducing information asymmetry and enjoy lower cost of capital (e.g., King, Pownall, and Waymire 1990; Coller and Yohn 1997; Verrecchia 2001). In addition, buy companies are able to do income increasing earnings management in order to meet forecasts. Therefore, they need to do less income decreasing FM than the sell companies.

Consistent with the expectation adjustment hypothesis, and assuming that the management seeks to align market expectations with their own (see Ajinkya and Gift1984), it is especially true when the management have extremely promising news to convey (Riley, 2007),and therefore, a favourable track record is most helpful for enhancing the forecast credibility of buy companies. This might be due to the fact that by conveying true information regarding their favourable records, buy companies' private information, which is usually promising, is fully impounded into their stock prices, and consequently, they are more capable of reducing information asymmetry to enjoy a lower cost of capital. This might be interpreted as buy companies conveying a less pessimistic forecast to the market (figure 5-1).

6.5.2 Behavior of Sell Companies

The findings of logistic regression, contingency table and analysis of variance for H1 showed that the sell companies produce more downward biased forecasts than buy companies (H1 supported).However, despite my previous expectation for hypothesis 2, the sell companies do not have higher positive forecasts errors than buy companies (H2 not supported). The reason for the downward forecasts management of the sell companies might be that they either like to manage analysts' forecasts (Cotter et al., 2006), or they are likely to avoid the unfavourable utility minimizing consequences of missing forecasts.

Following the Private Securities Litigation Reform Act of 1995, that proves to be more onerous for plaintiffs that are trying to prove misrepresentation (Rogers and Stocken 2005), companies have more space to choose whether to report imprecise forecasts. In addition, Stunda (2008) provides evidence that after SOX (2002) regulation, companies tend to exert greater downward forecasts management. There have been many researches that show the management issues imprecise forecasts to guide the analysts' forecasts downward (Libby, Hunton, Tan, & Seybert, 2008); (Cotter et al., 2006), or to favourably affect the stock price (Athanasakou et al., 2009; Kim & Shi, 2011). This might be explained for observing not for a higher rate of positive forecasts errors in sell companies compared to buy companies, despite the fact that they produce more downward biased forecasts compared to their buy counterparts. The reason for downward forecasts management of sell companies might be that they want to manage the analysts' forecasts downward.

However, the findings of H3 and H5 show that forecasts errors that are calculated using unbiased forecasts are more negative than forecast errors that are calculated by using issued forecasts. The implications of the findings about H3 and H5 are that sell companies not only do downward forecasts management

250

to guide the analysts' forecasts downward, but they also do downward forecasts management to avoid market punishments that results from missing forecasts (Beyer, 2006; Li & Ding, 2008). The reason for this is that as mentioned in Chapter 2, sell companies do not usually enjoy high economic profit. Therefore, the pessimistic forecasts of sell companies are to avoid market punishments, rather than being opportunistic. Such behaviour by the sell companies could be consistent with the notion of the prospect theory, in which instead of scrutiny in the company's financial information, investors use heuristics measures, such as earnings forecasts errors to analyse the financial information of the company.

On the other hand, according to Dutta and Gigler (2002) framework, the pessimistic forecasts of the sell companies might not be because of opportunism. Such pessimism makes their reporting process consistent with the efficiency perspective that corresponds with the revelation principle. Therefore, consistent with Dutta and Gigler's (2006) proposition, conducting income increasing earnings management is potentially costly for sell (non-growth) companies. Hence, they do not report delusive optimistic forecasts (see proposition 3 of Dutta and Gigler (2006)). The heavy costs of issuing optimistic forecasts and consequently losing those forecasts come in the form of litigation, contract termination and takeover (Beniluz, 2007; Frost, 1997; Kim & Shi, 2011).

6.5.3 Interpreting the Optimistic and Pessimistic Forecasts

As was mentioned earlier in Chapter 1, there are two different approaches regarding forecast issuance. The first approach is that management's forecasts consist of biased signals, and the management will use earnings and forecasts management as tools to create positive earnings surprise that will lead to a temporary stock price appreciation or prevent stock price depreciation. This view corresponds with the opportunistic perspective of the positive accounting theory. The second approach believes that by providing accurate forecasts, the management provides the correct information to the market, therefore, their forecasts are truthful. This view corresponds to the efficiency perspective of the positive accounting theory.

According to Abarbanell and Lehavy (2003b),buy companies conduct income increasing earnings management, whereas sell companies do not possess enough resources and have less accounting flexibility to do that (Su, 2005). The finding of this research for H1 is that buy companies issue less pessimistic (or more optimistic) forecasts than sell companies. The finding of this research for H1 is consistent with Abarbanell and Lehavy (2003b) framework, in which buy (growth) companies issue optimistic forecasts and conduct income increasing earnings management to reach forecasts and produce positive earnings surprises.

In addition, the findings of this research for H1 show that sell companies issue more pessimistic (less optimistic) forecasts than buy companies. Based on Dutta and Gigler (2002) proposition, since missing the forecasts unfavourably affects the management utilities, both buy and sell companies avoid doing so.

Furthermore, the findings of this research for H3 show that, in sell group companies, the companies that meet forecasts have higher negative forecasts management than the companies that miss forecasts.

Since sell companies do not have enough resources, which makes them constrained in effectively manipulating the profit (Howell, 2012), it is predicted that sell companies produce downward biased forecasts (issue pessimistic forecasts) in order to avoid missing forecasts. Producing downward biased forecasts in sell companies was further examined by testing the difference in the frequency of negative/positive forecasts errors between the forecasts errors that are calculated by using the "unmanaged" and issued forecasts (H5). The findings support (H5). The findings of the test state that the forecasts errors that are calculated by using "unmanaged" forecasts are more negative than the forecasts errors that are calculated by using issued forecasts. This shows that the sell companies only do downward forecasts management to reach to forecasts and produce positive forecasts errors.

The difference in the forecasts management of the buy and sell companies might explain the difference in approaches for efficiency (non-pessimistic) and opportunistic (pessimistic) forecasts.

Following the framework that was developed by Dutta and Gigler (2002), in which earnings forecasts assists in the process of transparent financial reporting, this research investigated the hypothesized effects of the analysts' recommendations on the forecast management. Consistent with the framework advocated by Dutta and Gigler (2002) and Abarbanell and Lehavy (2003b),this research shows that buy companies conduct income increasing earnings management to avoid negative forecasts errors, while sell companies produce downward biased forecasts (H1 supported) to avoid negative earnings surprise (H3 and H5 supported), and its consequent market punishments that unfavourably affects the management's utility. This research adds to the literature by finding an additional factor that affects the management's decisions toward issuing forecasts. It has been found that companies' growth status represented by analysts' recommendations can affect the management's decision to conduct forecasts management.

Therefore, consistent with Dutta and Gigler's (2002) proposition for sell companies, it is optimal to make earnings management potentially costly for managers, so that they do not have delusive optimistic forecasts (see proposition 3 of Dutta and Gigler 2002).

6.6   Interpretations of the Findings

In this research, even though it is discovered that the managers of sell companies use downward forecast management (H1 supported) to produce positive forecasts errors (H3 and H5 supported), Wang (2003) suggests that this would only have a short increasing effect on the market, as investors will learn of this fact from the past financial statements of the company. And if a manager repeats such an action for a number of times, the investors will lose their trust in the company. But as far as short term benefit is concerned, the management perceives the increases quite favourably, and this scenario will hold.

The results agree with those from other researches in forecasts management and forecasts errors contexts. The results extends previous researches with regards to the effect that financial reporting has on the market value (Lev & Zarowin, 1999). It is suggested that not only the financial information affects the market value of the company, but the market perception about the company will invariably affect the accuracy of voluntary information disclosure. This was accomplished by seeing that sell and buy companies have different strategies toward precision of managers' forecasts. Moreover, the findings of this study is consistent with the result of Feng and Koch (2010),which shows that the company that possesses large analysts' forecast error increases the frequencies of forecasts in order to decrease information asymmetry.

The result is consistent with Matsumoto (2002), who suggests that the stock market can function as an incentive that affect forecast management. In addition, the results also complement Abarbanell & Lehavy (2003b) framework, in which the market incentives affect the motivation of managers to conduct earnings management. The Abarbanell and Lehavy (2003b) shows that buy companies do income increasing earnings management to reach to forecasts and produce positive forecasts errors. Since the buy companies have ample resources to manipulate the profit, there is less communication restriction for them and the revelation principle holds for them (Dutta and Gigler 2002).

However, Abarbanell and Lehavy (2003b) suggest that the sell companies do not have enough resources to do income increasing earnings management. The restrictions of the resources come in the form of lack of new products, and lack of profitable investment opportunities. In addition, sell companies face restrictions in manipulating the profit, as they do not seem to have new markets and high prospective return. Furthermore, the sell company's stock price sensitivity to earnings news is not high (Abarbanell and Lehavy, 2003b).

Such obligations restrict the sell companies from communicating the full dimensionality of their information set to the market. If "unmanaged" earnings contain noises that the manager can observe, it is difficult for them to take action and manipulate the profit and to remove the noises. Thus, the lack of resources will render the sell companies unable to communicate the full dimensionality of their rich information set to investors through the manipulation of reported earnings.

Therefore, the communication restrictions that the sell companies have, relate to the ability of the manager to correctly communicate their information. For that reason, sell companies are expected to have different approaches in conveying information to investors compared to buy companies. Thus, according to Evans and Sridhar (2010), in case of the sell companies, it is possible for non-truthful reporting to occur. This study adds to this framework by suggesting that, when the company does not have enough resources to conduct earnings management (Su 2005), it will pursue forecasts management instead.

According to Dye (2008), Evans and Sridhar (2009), and Demski (1998) since in case of sell companies the agent is unable to perfectly communicate their private information, they might commit to less truthful reporting.

The overall empirical evidence also complements the implication in Kasznik (1999a) and Matsumoto (2002) by suggesting that the incentive to manage earnings and forecasts may not be identical in all companies. The empirical evidence suggests that discontinuities around zero in the forecasts errors distributions is driven by forecasts management, is, at least partly, under the influence of companies' financial situation, which is presented by the analysts' recommendations.

The findings about the relationship of forecasts management and forecasts errors in buy and sell companies is consistent with the findings of Savov (2006),which suggest that companies that are overvalued present a stronger influence of fundamental earnings over reporting bias. This is true because, while I showed that sell companies produce downward biased forecasts to meet forecasts and produce positive forecasts errors, Abarbanell and Lehavy (2003b) showed that buy companies do income increasing earnings management to reach to the forecasts and produce positive earnings surprises. Therefore, since buy companies are usually overvalued, their reporting is more biased toward increasing the profit.

6.7   Importance of the Findings

The findings are consistent with the result of previous researches, in that managers anticipate that the market will react differently when the forecasts are missed, versus when they are (just) met, and that the management undertake actions to meet the forecasts in order to boost the stock market status of the company (McVa, Nagar, & Tang, 2006). The importance of these findings is that they show analysts' recommendations in terms of buying or selling of the stocks might have informational value that can be used by individual investors to assess the quality of managers' forecasts. In addition, the results obtained here would be useful for future theory development.

6.8   Contribution of the Study

The contribution of this study is that it tests the framework that was developed by Dutta and Gigler (2002). An important attribute of this framework is that the revelation principle holds. The following paragraphs explain both the theoretical and practical contributions of the findings.

6.8.1   Theoretical Contributions of the Study

Previous findings indicate that the management manages the forecasts downward, so that reported earning meets them, and causes positive earnings surprises (Bartov et al., 2002; Downing & Sharpe, 2003). On the contrary, other researchers contend that the undesirable consequences of producing downward biased forecasts (like share price decline that follows the reduce in forecasts) is stronger than the desirable effects of positive earnings surprises

(Bernhardt & Campello, 2007). It is suggested that ignoring the financial situations of the companies is the main reason behind the controversy between undesirable and desirable consequences of producing downward biased forecasts. When the stocks recommendations are on the buy or on the sell, implications are abound on whether the management is motivated enough to produce downward biased forecast by meeting forecasts produce positive earnings surprises. However, as per Bernhardt and Campello (2005) suggestion, it is perceived that for buy companies, the negative effect of producing downward biased forecasts is far greater than the positive effect of meeting forecasts. So, the companies that are classified as the Buy conduct income-increasing earnings management instead of producing downward biased forecast.

The findings of this research add to the literature by proving that not only the buy companies (which are supposed to be growth companies) engage in income increasing earnings management to achieve positive forecast error (Burgstahler & Dichev, 1997; Libby et al., 2008; Watts & Zimmerman, 1990), but sell (non-growth) companies engage in negative forecast management to accomplish the same goal as well. Fitting to the framework of Abarbanell and Lehavy (2003b),where buy companies engage in income increasing earnings management to meet or beat forecasts and consistent with Brown (2001) and Burgstahler & Eames (2002) and Matsumoto (2002), this study shows that sell companies produce downward biased forecasts in order to meet or beat the forecasts. In addition, the findings suggest that studying forecasts errors along with forecasts management might be more illustrative than studying forecasts errors and forecasts management separately.

The secondary contribution of the findings of this study is that it examines the consistency of several forecasts management measurement models, including those developed by Wang (2003), Burgestahler and Eams (2005) and Matsumoto (2002). Since I observed a negative kink in the distribution of forecasts management on the right side of the positive forecasts errors, and since there is justifiable relationship between the forecasts management and forecasts errors, it can be surmised that Burgestahler and Eams (2005) and Matsumoto (2002) forecasts management measurement models are consistent. On top of that, since the findings fit in to the framework developed by previous researches in the case of direction of forecasts and earnings management (Conlisk, 1996; Demski, 1998; Kaiser, 1974; Watts & Zimmerman, 1990), it provides a solid evidence that Burgestahler and Eams (2005) and Matsumoto (2002) models are viable and valid.

This study helps to understand the mixed findings in the managers' forecasts literature. While the previous studies suggested that managers' forecasts are opportunistic, and the management uses the forecasts to manage the analysts' forecasts (Cotter et al., 2006; Desai et al., 2004) and affect the stock prices (Athanasakou et al., 2009), there are several other studies that show that since the management's forecast conveys insider information to the outsiders, it helps decrease information asymmetry, hence decreasing the costly litigation of stockholders versus the company (Beyer, 2006; Li & Ding, 2008). It also helps the company to have transparent and clear financial reporting (Bartov & Cohen, 2008; Hirst et al., 1999). This study adds to the mixed findings in the literature, by showing that management's forecasts contain bias that is predictable, considering the analysts' recommendations about the company. In other words, sell companies' forecasts are more pessimistically biased than buy companies' forecasts.

The findings introduce analysts' recommendation as a new variable that can predict the direction of forecasts management. The findings of this study indicate that the opportunistic forecasts are more likely when the company is in the sell recommendation. The relationship between the analysts' recommendations and forecasts management has not been thoroughly investigated in previous literature.

This study addresses the need for research regarding the interaction between elements of the financial reporting such as earnings and forecasts management. This need was brought up in a literature review article (Hirst et al., 2008; Riley, 2007). I interpret the results as the growth and non-growth companies pursuing different strategies to meet forecasts and produce positive earnings surprises. When the companies are in a growth situation, they issue optimistic forecasts and pursue income increasing earnings management to achieve those forecasts afterward (Abarbanell and Lehavy 2003b). On the other hand, when the companies are in a distressed situation, they issue pessimistic forecasts so that they can avoid the undesirable consequences of negative earnings surprise at the earnings' announcement date.

6.8.2   Practical Contributions of the Study

This research is practically useful, as it addresses the need for further research on the characteristics of the forecasts that was highlighted by Hirst et al. (2008). The findings extend the existing knowledge regarding the information content of the forecasts that affect the financial information of the users' decisions. This study also helps to provide a better understanding of the role that forecasts management plays in decreasing forecasts errors. The findings warn investors to carefully evaluate the management and analysts'[1] forecasts before they form their expectations about the company. This is especially imperative when there is great temptation in the market for the sale of the company's stocks. In addition, the implications for standard setting is that the forecasts of buy and sell companies possesses different levels of credibility.

Models that included is closure choices along with other (real) choices or effort allocation provide us a improved perception concerning how the companies' disclosure records influence not only market estimates, but also companies' other (real) choices and cash flows, along with the wellbeing of diverse shareholder groups (Kanodia, 2007). Obviously, including such actual choices in voluntary disclosure models adds a further level of complication. However, the understandings that can possibly be achieved regarding the interdependencies among disclosures, cash flow distributions, and the welfare of stakeholders make such models worth the attempt (Riley, 2007).

---

[1] According to Baginski et al. (2011) and Choi et al. (2010) analysts' forecasts are highly under the influence of management forecasts. The reason is that, the main source of the analysts to form expectation about the companies' future profit is the company's own earnings' predictions or "guidance" (Williams 1996; Burgstahler and Eames 2006; Baginski and Hassell 1990; Hutton et al. 2012; Cotter et al. 2010).

6.9   Suggestions

6.9.1   Practical Suggestions

This study cautions investors and analysts to carefully evaluate the managers' forecasts before using it to form their expectations vis-à-vis the company's future performance, especially when there is great temptation in the market for the sale of the company's stocks.

The information about the analysts' recommendations might contain important implications for forecasts management, as they might convey a great informational value that can be used by researchers or even investors, and carry clues for interpreting the invisible implications of the stocks.

It is suggested that standard setters and regulators pay great attention to the implications of the analysts' recommendations and keep greater surveillance, via stricter restrictions, over earnings projections of the companies that do not have a satisfactory stock market status.

6.9.2   Suggestions for Future Research

The findings of this research is in contrast with the result of Campello (2010), who found that the negative influence of downward forecast revisions on stock price overlooks the stock price rise after the earnings announcement. Further researches need to be conducted to see whether price reduction effect of producing downward biased forecasts will outweigh the positive price effect of meeting and beating forecasts. If it is true, then the future researchers should addressthe situations that make the negative consequences of producing downward biased forecasts to outweigh the future positive effects of meeting or beating forecasts, and why the management conduct downward forecast management in such situations.

6.10 Limitations

The limitations that this study dealt with are explained as follows:

There are a number of disadvantages in using the analysts' recommendations as an indicator for market growth. First, according to Stickel (1995), the reaction of investors to analysts' recommendations, and consequently, its effect on stock prices, are influenced by several factors such as the size of the brokerage firm, the size of the recommended company, the reputation of the analysts and the magnitude of the change in recommendation, the strength of the recommendation, and the marketing ability of the brokerage house issuing the recommendation. However, when consensus analysts' recommendations are considered, such influences and their abnormal effects will be alleviated.

The second disadvantage of the analysts' recommendations is that some analysts maintain on-going relationships with specific companies (e.g. conducting investment banking for the companies (Dugar & Nathan, 1995; Feng & Koch, 2010; Matsumoto, 2002). For example, Michaely and Womack (1999) show that the recommendations by an underwriter analysts showed a significant evidence of bias. Moreover, to some extent, the investors understand this bias, and they place more value on the information released by independent analysts (Chang, Ng, & Yu, 2008), and as a result of this, the analysts' recommendation and the real market trend might not be completely similar (Jegadeesh & Kim, 2010). Problems such as these are growing, especially with the fact that some small companies are followed by only a small number of analysts'. In addition, the analysts' recommendations includes some analysts' optimism anomaly, which were documented by Francis and Philbrick (1993). However, by considering consensus analysts' recommendations, such influences and their abnormal effects are minimized. In addition, by excluding the information of the companies that are followed by only a few analysts' from the sample the abnormal effects of analysts' bias is minimized.

The other limitation is that the study sampling covers only the years 2009 and 2010,which are after immediate recovery from financial crises. The financial situation of the companies just after recovery could possibly affect the management's behaviour.

Finally, since Matsumoto proposed measure of forecasts management as a measurement tool for the analysts' forecasts, if market is inefficient, then the information of the analysts and management might differ. Therefore, the model might not fully capture the management's forecasts management. However, as Li & Ding (2008), Castura et al. (2010), and Correia et al. (2010) documented, since NYSE stock market is efficient, it might not cause serious problem to the reliability of the results. Other models of measuring forecasts management might not be as efficient. Although they are tried to be comprehensive and included all of the known components of managers' forecasts, some of the hidden effects might have been missed entirely.

6.11 Conclusion

This chapter briefly summarized the research objectives and the overall results of the study. In line with this, the strategies of the management have been viewed vis-à-vis reporting earnings forecasts, aided by theories that have been presented in the theoretical framework (Chapter 2). The practical and theoretical implications of the study have also been highlighted, and recommendations were made to improve the accuracy of the managers' forecasts, along with how investors and analysts could adjust the optimism and pessimism of managers' forecasts.

This thesis highlights previous findings related to the concepts of forecasts optimism and pessimism. It has also fills the probable gaps regarding characteristics of managers' forecasts that highlighted by Hirst et al. (2008) and lack of research about determinant of management precision (optimism/pessimism) that was highlighted by (Hong & Kacperczyk, 2010),that have existed along the way. Investigating the effect of analysts' recommendations on the accuracy of managers' forecasts did this.

In addition, the discrepancies that existed between the previous and current findings have been duly clarified. The discrepancy was the lack of consistency in the result of past researches, regarding the producing downward biased forecasts to produce positive earnings surprises. Some researches emphasize that, the undesirable stock price decline consequences of producing downward biased forecasts overweight the positive stock price effect of producing positive earnings surprises (Su, 2005). On the other hand, other researches claim that management does downward forecasts management to produce positive earnings surprises (Matsumoto, 2002; Burgstahler and Eams, 2006). In this study, I showed that, although for buy companies the undesirable stock price decline consequences of producing downward biased forecasts overweight the positive stock price effect of producing positive earnings surprises, since the stock price of the sell companies is less susceptible to earnings news, the undesirable price consequences of producing downward biased forecasts is not high for sell companies. Therefore, sell companies do downward forecasts management to produce positive earnings surprise.

Consequently, the researcher believes that the results of the present work contribute to a better understanding of the reliability of managers' forecasts that has attracted a lot of researchers in recent years. Much of the research has attempted to caution against the employment of pessimistic forecasts in many contexts, and to argue in favor of optimistic forecasts.

However, the results of this study showed that when the company is non-affluent and where the management faces difficulties in manipulating the reported profit, they tend to manipulate the forecasts in order to avoid the negative earnings surprises. The results of the study also show that in the present state of affairs, pessimistic forecasts may not necessarily reflect the opportunism, and it could be fitted into the framework, in which forecasts as voluntary disclosure and reported profit as mandatory disclosure could contribute to a more efficient financial reporting.

According to Dutta and Gigler (2002) as long as communication restrictions such as regulatory limitations do not restrict the management to follow different earnings management or forecasts management strategies to meet their own forecasts, earnings and forecasts management could be beneficial. An implication of the present study is that, ideally, depending on the financial affluence of the company, both the optimistic and pessimistic forecast could contribute in conveying richer information to the market. Where pessimistic forecast has more to contribute to convey a bad situation of the company and optimistic forecast has more shares in conveying the good news of the company. It is hoped that the results will prove useful to all stakeholders involved in voluntary disclosure.

While the present study reveals some significant points in terms of reliability of managers' forecasts, the findings should neither be overestimated nor underestimated. Gathering data from different markets and from different time periods may shed more light on the issue of reliability of managers' forecasts.

APPENDICES

APPENDIX I

Table of rotated component matrix for calculation of the variable Difficulty by using the five items of Lag_loss, Predict_loss, STDAF, STDAFE, Spread, STD_RET. The first component is used as measure for difficulty.

Rotated Component Matrix

	Component		
	1	2	3
Lag_loss	0.180	0.106	0.780
Predict_loss	-0.58	0.896	0.060
STDAF	-0.51	0.107	-0.669
STDAFE	0.963	-0.005	0.089
Spread	0.838	0.554	-0.159
STD_RET	0.960	-0.041	0.090

REFERENCES

Abarbanell, J., & Lehavy, R. (2003a). Biased forecasts or biased earnings? The role of reported earnings in explaining apparent bias and over/underreaction in analysts' earnings forecasts. *Journal of Accounting and Economics, 36*, 105-146.

Abarbanell, J., & Lehavy, R. (2003b). Can stock recommendations predict earnings management and analysts' forcast errors. *Journal of Accounting Research 41*, 1-31.

Ahmed, A. S., Billings, B. K., & Morton, R. M. (2004). Extreme Accruals, Earnings Quality, and Investor Mispricing. Texas A&M University - Mays Business School.

Ajinkya, B., Bhojraj, S., & Sengupta, P. (2005). The association between outside directors, institutional investors and the properties of management earnings forecasts. *Journal of Accounting Research, 43*(3), 343–376.

Ajinkya, B. B., & Gift, M. J. (1984). Corporate managers' earnings forecasts and symmetrical adjustments of market expectations. *Journal of Accounting Research, 22*(2), 425-444.

Albring, S., Banyi, M., Dhaliwal, D. S., & Pereira, R. (2008). *The influence of Reg'ulation Fair Disclosure on firm financing decisions*: Working Paper, University of Arizonao. Document Number)

Arel, B., Beaudoin, C., & Cianci, A. (2011). The impact of ethical leadership and the internal audit function on financial reporting decisions. *Available at SSRN 1756284.*

Arping, S., & Sautner, Z. (2010). The effect of corporate governance regulation on transparency: evidence from the Sarbanes-Oxley Act of 2002. *Social Science Research Network, 12*(540), 1344-1373.

Arya, A., Glover, J., & Sunder, S. (1998). Earnings management and the revelation principle. *Review of Accounting Studies, 3*, 7-34.

Asare, K. N. (2009). *Essays on the influence of corporate governance on financial analysts' forecast-related judgments*: Bentley University.

Athanasakou, V. E., Strong, N. C., & Walker, M. (2009). Earnings management or forecast guidance to meet analyst expectations? *Accounting and Business Research, 39*(1), 3-35.

Baginski, S., Hassell, J., & Waymire, G. (1994). Some evidence on the news content of preliminary earnings estimates. *Accounting Review*, 265-273.

Baginski, S. P. (1987). Intraindustry information transfers associated with management forecasts of earnings. *Journal of Accounting Research, 25*(2), 196-216.

Baginski, S. P., & Hassell, J. M. (1990). The market interpretation of management earnings forecasts as a predictor of subsequent financial analyst forecast revision. *Accounting Review, 65*(1), 175-190.

Baginski, S. P., Hassell, J. M., & Wieland, M. M. (2011). An examination of the effects of management earnings forecast form and explanations on financial analyst forecast revisions. *Advances in Accounting, 27*(1), 17-25.

Baik, B., & Jiang, G. (2006). The use of management forecasts to dampen analysts' expectations. *Journal of Accounting and Public Policy, 25*(5), 531-553.

Bailey, W., Li, H., Mao, C. X., & Zhong, R. (2003). Regulation Fair Disclosure and Earnings Information: Market, Analyst, and Corporate Responses. *The Journal of Finance., 58* (6), 2487-2514.

Bartlett, M. S. (1954). A note on the multiplying factors for various X2 approximations. *Journal of the Royal Statistical Society. Series B (Methodological), 16*(2), 296-298.

Bartov, E., & Cohen, D. A. (2008). The 'Numbers Game' in The Pre-and Post-Sarbanes-Oxley Eras

Bartov, E., Givoly, D., & Hayn, C. (2002). The rewards to meeting or beating earnings expectations. *Journal of Accounting and Economics, 33*, 173-204.

Barua, A., Legoria, J., & Moffitt, J. S. (2006). Accruals Management to Achieve Earnings Benchmarks: A Comparison of Preâ€‑managed Profit and Loss Firms. *Journal of Business Finance & Accounting, 33*(5 & 6), 653-670.

Beaver, W., McNichols, M. F., & Nelson, K. K. (2006). An Alternative Interpretation of the Discontinuity in Earnings Distributions. Stanford University.

Bebchuk, L., & Grinstein, Y. (2005). The Growth of Executive Pay. *Oxford Review of Economic Policy, 21* (2), 283-303.

Beniluz, Y. (2007). Management earnings forecasts and simultaneous release of earnings news. *Unpublished Working Paper. Rutgers, The State University of New Jersey.*

Bennett, B. K., & Bradbury, M. E. (2010). An analysis of the reasons for the asymmetries surrounding earnings benchmarks. *Accounting & Finance, 50*(3), 529–554.

Bergman, N., & Roychowdhury, S. (2007). Investor Sentiment, Expectations, and Corporate Disclosure. MIT Sloan School of Management.

Bergstresser, D., & Philippon, T. (2006). CEO incentives and earnings management. *Journal of Financial Economics, 80*(3), 511-529.

Bernhardt, D., & Campello, M. (2002). The dynamics of earnings forecast management.

Bernhardt, D., & Campello, M. (2007). The dynamics of earnings forecast management. *Review of Finance, 11*(2), 287-324.

Beyer, A. (2006). *Essays on earnings forecasts, earnings management and capital market prices.* Northwestern University.

Beyer, A. (2008). Financial analysts' forecast revisions and managers' reporting behavior *Journal of Accounting and Economics, 46*(2-3), 334-348.

Beyer, A. (2009). Capital market prices, management forecasts, and earnings management. *The Accounting Review, 84*(6), 1713-1747.

Beyer, A., Cohen, D. A., Lys, T. Z., & Walther, B. R. (2010). The financial reporting environment: Review of the recent literature. *Journal of Accounting and Economics, 50*(2), 296-343.

Bird, R., McElwee, B., & McKinnon, J. (2000). A Global Perspective of Analysts' Earnings Forecasts. *The Journal of Investing, 9*(4), 76-82.

Bowen, R. M., DuCharme, L., & Shores, D. (1995). Stakeholders' implicit claims and accounting method choice. *Journal of Accounting and Economics, 20*(3), 255-295.

Brown, L. (2001). A temporal analysis of earnings surprises: profit versus loss. *Journal of Accounting Research, 39*(2), 173-204.

Brown, L. D., & Caylor, M. L. (2005). A Temporal Analysis of Quarterly Earnings Thresholds: Propensities and Valuation Consequences. *The Accounting Review, 80*(2), 423-440.

Brown, L. D., & Pinello, A. S. (2005). Do Managers Trade Off Expectations Management for Earnings Management? Georgia State University

Brushko, I. (2013). Financial Signaling and Earnings Forecasts.

Bundy, H. H. (2007). Aligning Management and Shareholder Interests. William Blair and Company L.L.C.

Burgstahler, D., & Dichev, I. (1997). Earnings management to avoid earnings decreases and losses. *Journal of Accounting and Economics, 24*(1), 99-126.

Burgstahler, D., & Eames, M. (2006). Management of Earnings and Analysts' Forecasts to Achieve Zero and Small Positive Earnings Surprises. *Journal of Business Finance & Accounting,, 33*(5 & 6), 633–652.

Burgstahler, D. C., & Eames, M. J. (2003). Earnings Management to Avoid Losses and Earnings Decreases: Are Analysts Fooled?*. *Contemporary Accounting Research, 20*(2), 253-294.

Bushee, B. J., Matsumoto, D. A., & Miller, G. S. (2004). Managerial and investor responses to disclosure regulation: The case of Reg FD and conference calls. *The Accounting Review, 79*(3), 617-643.

Campello, D. B. M. (2010). The Dynamics of Earnings Forecast Management. University of Illinois

Canace, T. G., Caylor, M. L., Johnson, P. M., & Lopez, T. J. (2010). The effect of Regulation Fair Disclosure on expectations management: International evidence. *Journal of Accounting and Public Policy, 29*(5), 403-423.

Cao, Z., & Narayanamoorthy, G. S. (2005). The Effect of Litigation Risk on Management Earnings Forecasts*. *Contemporary Accounting Research, 28*(1), 125-173.

Castura, J., Litzenberger, R., Gorelick, R., & Dwivedi, Y. (2010). Market Efficiency and Microstructure Evolution in U.S. Equity Markets: A High-Frequency Perspective. RGM Advisors, LLC.

Caylor, M. L., Lopez, T. J., & Rees, L. (2007). Is the value relevance of earnings conditional on the timing of earnings information? *Journal of Accounting and Public Policy, 26*(1), 62-95.

Caylor, M. L., T. J. Lopez, & Rees, L. (2003). Does the timing of earnings information disclosure during a quarter influence firm value? Georgia State University and Texas A&M University.

Chan, H., Faff, R., Mather, P., & Ramsay, A. (2012). The association between directors' independence, reputation and management earnings forecasts. University of Melbourne.

Chang, M., Ng, J., & Yu, K. (2008). The influence of analyst and management forecasts on investor decision making: an experimental approach. *Australian Journal of Management, 33*(1), 47-67.

Chen, Q., Francis, J., & Jiang, W. (2005). Investor learning about analyst predictive ability. *Journal of Accounting and Economics, 39*(1), 3-24.

Chen, Q., Kelly, K., & Salterio, S. E. (2011). Do changes in audit actions and attitudes consistent with increased auditor scepticism deter aggressive earnings management? An experimental investigation. *Accounting, Organizations and Society, 37*(2), 95-116.

Chen, Z., Dhaliwal, D. S., & Xie, H. (2010). Regulation Fair Disclosure and the cost of equity capital. *Review of Accounting Studies, 15*(1), 106-144.

Cheng, Q., Luo, T., & Yue, H. (2013). Managerial Incentives and Management Forecast Precision. *Available at SSRN 2202064.*

Cheong, F. S., & Thomas, J. (2013). *Revisiting the anomalous distributions of EPS forecast errors*: Working paper, Rutgers University and Yale Universityo. Document Number)

Chin, C. L., Kleinman, G., Lee, P., & Lin, M. F. (2006). Corporate ownership structure and accuracy and bias of mandatory earnings forecast: Evidence from Taiwan. *Journal of International Accounting Research, 5*(2), 41-62.

Choi, J., Myers, L., Zang, Y., & Ziebart, D. (2006). The roles that forecast surprise and forecast error play in determining management forecast precision. Seoul National University.

Chua, W. F. (1986). Radical developments in accounting thought. *Accounting Review, 17*, 601-632.

Clarkson, P. M., Dontoh, A., Richardson, G., & Sefcik, S. E. (1992). The Inclusion of Earnings Forecasts In IPO Prospectuses. *Contemporary Accounting Research, 8*(2), 601-626.

Coase, R. H. (1937). The Nature of the Firm. *Economica 4*(16), 386-405.

Cohen, L., Marcus, A. J., Rezaee, Z., & Tehranian, H. (2011). Earnings Guidance, Earnings Management, and Share Prices.

Coller, M., & Yohn, T. L. (1997). Management Forecasts and Information Asymmetry: An Examination of Bid-Ask Spreads. *Journal of Accounting Research, 35*(2), 181-191.

Committee on Capital Markets Regulation, Interim report of the Committee on Capital Markets Regulation. (2006). from http://www.capmktsreg.org/research.html

Conlisk, J. (1996). Why Bounded Rationality? *Journal of Economic Literature, June*, 669-700.

Cooper, D. R., Schindler, P. S., & Sun, J. (2003). Business research methods.

Copeland, R. M., & Marioni, R. J. (1972). Executives' forecasts of earnings per share versus forecasts of naive models. *The Journal of Business, 45*(4), 497-512.

Cormier, D., & Martinez, I. (2006). The association between management earnings forecasts, earnings management, and stock market valuation: Evidence from French IPOs. *The International Journal of Accounting, 41* 209-236.

Cornell, B., & Shapiro, A. C. (1987). Corporate stakeholders and corporate finance. *Financial management*, 5-14.

Correia, C., Flynn, D., Uliana, E., & Wormald, M. (2010). *Financial Management*. Berkeley: Juta & Co.

Cotter, J., Tuna, I., & Wysocki, P. D. (2006). Expectations management and beatable targets: How do analysts react to public earnings guidance? . *Contemporary Accounting Research, 23*(3), 593-624.

Cotter, J., Tuna, I., & Wysocki, P. D. (2010). Expectations Management and Beatable Targets: How Do Analysts React to Explicit Earnings Guidance?*. *Contemporary Accounting Research, 23*(3), 593-624.

Coulton, J., Taylor, S. J., & Taylor, S. L. (2005). Is 'Benchmark Beating' by Australian Firms Evidence of Earnings Management? *Accounting and Finance, 45*(4), 553-576.

Dambra, M., Wasley, C. E., & Wu, J. S. (2012). Soft-Talk Management Cash Flow Forecasts: Bias, Quality, and Stock Price Effects*. *Contemporary Accounting Research.*

Darke, P., Shanks, G., & Broadbent, M. (1998). Successfully completing case study research: combining rigour, relevance and pragmatism. *Information Systems Journal, 8*(4), 273-289.

Das, S., Kim, K., & Patro, S. (2010). An Examination of the Disagreements in Earnings Forecasts between Managers and Analysts Working Paper.

Das, S., Kyonghee, K., & Sukesh, P. (2008). An Analysis of Managerial Use and Market Consequences of Earnings Management and Expectation Management (Publication., from AAA 2009 Financial Accounting and Reporting Section (FARS) Paper. Available at SSRN: http://ssrn.com/abstract=1270841:

Dasgupta, P., Hammond, P., & Maskin, E. (1979). The implementation of social choice rules: some results on incentive compatibility. *Review of Economic Studies, 46*, 185-216.

DeAngelo, L. E. (1988). Managerial competition, information costs and corporate governance: the use of accounting performance measures in proxy contests. *Journal of Accounting and Economics, 10*, 3-36.

Dechow, P., Richardson, S., & Tuna, I. (2003). Why are earnings kinky? An examination of the earnings management explanation. *Review of Accounting Studies, 8*, 355-384.

Deegan, C., & Unerman, J. (Eds.). (2006). *Financial Accounting Theory*. London: The McGrow-Hill Companies.

Demers, E., & Vega, C. (2013). Understanding the Role of Managerial Textual Content in the Price Formation Process. University of Virginia.

Demski, J. (1998). Performance Measure Manipulation. *Contemporary Accounting Research, 15* 261-285.

Demski, J., & Frimor, H. (1999). Performance Measure Garbling Under Renegotiation in Multi-period Agencies. *Journal of Accounting Research, 37* 187-214.

Desai, H., Rajgopal, S., & Venkatachalam, M. (2004). Value-Glamour and Accruals Mispricing: One Anomaly or Two? *The Accounting Review* 355-385.

Dhaliwal, D. S., Lamoreaux, P. T., Lennox, C. S., & Mauler, L. M. (2014). Management Influence on Auditor Selection and Subsequent Impairments of Auditor Independence during the post SOX Period. *Contemporary Accounting Research*.

Dhole, S., Mishra, S., & Sivaramakrishnan, S. (2010). Benchmark for Earnings Performance: Management Forecasts Versus Analysts' Forecasts. *Available at SSRN 1598439*.

Diamond, D., & Verrecchia, R. (1991). Disclosure, liquidity, and the cost of capital. *The Journal of Finance, 66*, 1325-1355.

Donaldson, W. H. (2005). Speech by SEC Chairman: Remarks before the Financial Services Roundtable. U.S. Securities and Exchange Commission. from http://www.sec.gov/news/speech/spch040105whd.htm.

Downing, C., & Sharpe, S. (2003). Getting Bad News Out Early: Does it Really Help Stock Prices? Federal Reserve.

Duarte, J., Han, X., Harford, J., & Young, L. (2008). Information asymmetry, information dissemination and the effect of regulation FD on the cost of capital. *Journal of Financial Economics, 87*(1), 24-44.

Dugar, A., & Nathan, S. (1995). The effect of investment banking relationships on financial analysts' earnings forecasts and investment recommendations*. *Contemporary Accounting Research, 12*(1), 131-160.

Durtschi, C., & Easton, P. (2005). Earnings Management? The Shapes of the Frequency Distributions of Earnings Metrics are Not Evidence Ipso Facto. *Journal of Accounting Research, 43*(4), 557-592.

Dutta, S., & Gigler, F. (2002). The effect of earnings forecasts on earnings management. *Journal of Accounting Research, 40*(3), 631-656.

Dye, R. (1983). Communication and Post-decision Information. *Journal ofAccountingResearch, 21*(2), 514-533.

Dye, R. (1988). Earnings Management in an Overlapping Generations Model. *Journal of Accounting Research, 26* 195-235.

Eleswarapu, V. R., Thompson, R., & Venkataraman, K. (2004). The impact of Regulation Fair Disclosure: Trading costs and information asymmetry. *Journal of Financial and Quantitative Analysis, 39*(02), 209-225.

Emami, M., Amini, A., & Emami, A. (2012). The Impact of Earnings Management and Expectations Management on the Usefulness of Earnings and Analyst Forecasts in Firm Valuation. *Available at SSRN 2067855.*

Epstein, L. G., & Schneider, M. (2008). Ambiguity, information quality, and asset pricing. *The Journal of Finance, 63*(1), 197-228.

Ettredge, M., Huang, Y., & Zhang, W. (2011). Restatement Disclosures and Management Earnings Forecasts. *Weining, Restatement Disclosures and Management Earnings Forecasts (January 17, 2)*.

Evans, J. H., & Sridhar, S. S. (1996). Multiple control systems, accrual accounting, and earnings management. *Journal of Accounting Research, 34*(1), 45-65.

Fabrigar, L. R., Wegener, D. T., MacCallum, R. C., & Strahan, E. J. (1999). Evaluating the use of exploratory factor analysis in psychological research. *Psychological methods, 4*(3), 272.

Fama, E. F. (1998). Market efficiency, long-term returns, and behavioral finance. *Journal of Financial Economics, 49*(3), 283-306.

Fang, V. W. (2009). The Role of Management Forecast Precision in Predicting Management Forecast Error. Rutgers University.

Farrell, G. (2005). *America Robbed Blind*: Wizard Academy Press.

Felleg, R., Moers, F., & Renders, A. (2012). Investor Reaction to Higher Earnings Management Incentives of Overoptimistic CEOs. *The Accounting Review, 85*(6), 1951-1984.

Feng, M., & Koch, A. S. (2010). Once bitten, twice shy: The relation between outcomes of earnings guidance and management guidance strategy. *The Accounting Review, 85*, 1951.

Francis, J., & Philbrick, D. (1993). Analysts' Decisions As Products of a Multi-Task Environment. *Journal of Accounting Research, 31*(2), 216-230.

Frankel, R., McNichols, M., & Wilson, G. P. (1995). Discretionary disclosure and external financing. *Accounting Review, 70,* 135-150.

Frost, C. (1997). Disclosure policy choices of U.K. firms receiving modified audit reports. *Journal of Accounting and Economics, 23*(2), 163–187.

Fuller, J., & Jensen, M. C. (2002). Just Say No to Wall Street: Putting a Stop to the Earnings Game. *Journal of Applied Corporate Finance, 14* (4), 41-46.

Gibbard, A. (1973). Manipulation of voting schemes: a general result. *Econometrica: Journal of the Econometric Society,* 587-601.

Gleason, C. A., & Mills, L. F. (2008). Evidence of differing market responses to beating analysts' targets through tax expense decreases. *Review of Accounting Studies, 13*(2), 295-318.

Gomes, A., Gorton, G., & Madureira, L. (2004). *SEC Regulation Fair Disclosure, information, and the cost of capital*: National Bureau of Economic Researcho. Document Number)

Gomes, A., Gorton, G., & Madureira, L. (2007). SEC Regulation Fair Disclosure, information, and the cost of capital. *Journal of Corporate Finance, 13*(2-3), 300-334.

Gong, G., Li, L. Y., & Xie, H. (2009). The Association between Management Earnings Forecast Errors and Accruals. *The Accounting Review, 84*(2), 497–530.

Graham, J. R., Harvey, C. R., & Rajgopal, S. (2005). The economic implications of corporate financial reporting. *Journal of Accounting and Economics, 40*(1-3), 3-73.

Hair, J. F., Black, W. C., Babin, B. J., Anderson, R. E., & Tatham, R. L. (2006). Multivariate Data Analysis Pearson Prentice Hall. *Upper Saddle River.*

Hall, B., & Leibman, J. (1998). Are CEOs Really Paid Like Bureaucrats? . *Quarterly Journal of Economics, 113* (3), 653-691.

Hassell, J. M., & Jennings, R. H. (1986). Relative Forecast Accuracy and the Timing of Earnings Forecast Announcements. *The Accounting Review, 61*(1), 58-75.

Healy, M., & Perry, C. (2000). Comprehensive criteria to judge validity and reliability of qualitative research within the realism paradigm. *Qualitative Market Research: An International Journal, 3*(3), 118-126.

Heflin, F., Kross, W., & Suk, I. (2012). The effect of Regulation FD on the properties of management earnings forecasts. *Journal of Accounting and Public Policy, 31*(2), 161-184.

Herrmann, D. R., Hope, O. K., & Thomas, W. B. (2008). International diversification and forecast optimism: The effects of Reg FD. *Accounting Horizons, 22*, 179.

Hirst, D. E., Koonce, L., & Miller, J. (1999). The joint effect of management's prior forecast accuracy and the form of its financial forecasts on investor judgment. *Journal of Accounting Research, 37*, 101-124.

Hirst, E., Koonce, L., & Venkataraman, S. (2008). Management earnings forecasts: A review and framework. *Accounting Horizons 22*(3), 315–338.

Hochberg, Y. V., Sapienza, P., & Rgensen, A. (2009). A Lobbying Approach to Evaluating the Sarbanes-Oxley Act of 2002. *Journal of Accounting Research, 47*(2), 519-583.

Holmstrom, B. (1977). *On incentives and control in organizations.* Stanford University.

Hong, H., & Kacperczyk, M. (2010). Competition and bias. *The Quarterly Journal of Economics, 125*(4), 1683-1725.

Hovland, C. I., & Pritzker, H. A. (1957). Extent of opinion change as a function of amount of change advocated. *The Journal of Abnormal and Social Psychology, 54*(2), 257.

Howell, D. C. (2012). *Statistical methods for psychology*: Wadsworth Publishing Company.

Hsu, H. C. (2011). Standardized Unexpected Earnings In The US Technology Sector. *International Business & Economics Research Journal (IBER), 1*(9).

Hui, K. W. (2012). Voluntary Disclosure during Credit Watches: Do Credit Rating Agencies Concern about Disclosure Quality?

Hui, K. W., Matsunaga, S., & Morse, D. (2009). The impact of conservatism on management earnings forecasts. *Journal of Accounting and Economics, 47*, 192–207.

Hurwitz, H. (2012). *Litigation Risk and the Optimism in Long-horizon Management Forecasts of Bad News and Good News.* Unpublished Ph.D., Columbia University, United States -- New York.

Hutton, A. P., Lee, L. F., & Shu, S. Z. (2012). Do managers always know better? The relative accuracy of management and analyst forecasts. *Journal of Accounting Research, 50*(5), 1217-1244.

Hutton, A. P., & Stocken, P. (2009). Prior Forecasting Accuracy and Investor Reaction to Management Earnings Forecasts. Boston College - Carroll School of Management.

Irani, A. J., & Karamanou, I. (2003). Regulation Fair Disclosure, Analyst Following, and Analyst Forecast Dispersion. *Accounting Horizons, 17* (1), 15-29.

Ivković, Z., & Jegadeesh, N. (2004). The timing and value of forecast and recommendation revisions. *Journal of Financial Economics, 73*(3), 433-463.

Jaggi, B., & Xin, H. (2012). Accounting Conservatism and Informative Management Earnings Forecasts. *Available at SSRN 2151029*.

Jain, P. K., Kim, J.-C., & Rezaee, Z. (2008). The Sarbanes-Oxley Act of 2002 and Market Liquidity. *Financial Review, 43*(3), 361-382.

Jegadeesh, N., & Kim, W. (2010). Do analysts herd? An analysis of recommendations and market reactions. *Review of Financial Studies, 23*(2), 901-937.

Jensen, M. C., & Meckling, W. H. (1976). Theory of the Firm: Managerial Behavior, Agency Costs and Ownership Structure *Journal of Financial Economics, 3*(4), 305-360.

Jog, V., & McConomy, B. J. (2003). Voluntary Disclosure of Management Earnings Forecasts in IPO Prospectuses. *Journal of Business Finance & Accounting,, 30*(1/2), 125-167.

Kahneman, D., & Tversky, A. (1979). Prospect theory: An analysis of decision under risk. *Econometrica: Journal of the Econometric Society*, 263-291.

Kaiser, H. F. (1974). An index of factorial simplicity. *Psychometrika, 39*(1), 31-36.

Kamar, E., Karaca-Mandic, P., & Talley, E. (2009). Going-private decisions and the Sarbanes-Oxley Act of 2002: A cross-country analysis. *Journal of Law, Economics, and Organization, 25*(1), 107-133.

Kanodia, C. (2007). Accounting Disclosure and Real Effects. *Foundations and Trends¹ in Accounting, 1*(3), 167-258.

Kaplan, S. E., & Ravenscroft, S. P. (2004). The reputation effects of earnings management in the internal labor market. *Business Ethics Quarterly*, 453-478.

Kasznik, R. (1999a). On the association between voluntary disclosure and earnings management. *Journal of Accounting Research, 57*(1), 57-81.

Kasznik, R. (1999b). On the relation between earnings management and corporate voluntary disclosure. *Journal of Accounting Research, 31*(1), 57-81.

Kasznik, R., & Lev, B. (1995). To warn or not to warn: Management disclosures in the face of an earnings surprise. *Accounting review*, 113-134.

Kasznik, R., & McNichols, M. F. (2002). Does meeting earnings expectations matter? Evidence from analyst forecast revisions and share prices. *Journal of Accounting Research, 40*(3), 727-759.

Kelly, B., & Ljungqvist, A. (2012). Testing asymmetric-information asset pricing models. *Review of Financial Studies, 25*(5), 1366-1413.

Kim, J. W., & Shi, Y. (2011). Voluntary disclosure and the cost of equity capital: Evidence from management earnings forecasts. *Journal of Accounting and Public Policy, 30*, 348–366.

Kim, K., Pandit, S., & Wasley, C. (2012). Aggregate Uncertainty and the Issuance of Management Earnings Forecasts. *UIC College of Business Administration Research Paper*(10-04).

King, R., G. Pownall, , & Waymire, G. (1990). Expectations Adjustment Via Timely Management Forecasts: Review, Synthesis, and Suggestions for Future Research. *Journal of accounting Literature, 9*, 113-144.

King, R., Pownall, G., & Waymire, G. (1990). Expectations adjustment via timely management forecasts: Review, synthesis, and suggestions for future research. *Journal of accounting Literature, 9*(1), 113-144.

Kinney, W., Burgstahler, D., & Martin, R. (2002). Earnings surprise "materiality" as measured by stock returns. *Journal of Accounting Research, 40*(5), 1297-1329.

Knauer, T., & Wömpener, A. (2011). Management Forecast Regulation and Practice in Germany–Firm and Auditor Perspectives. *Accounting in Europe, 8*(2), 185-209.

Koch, A. (2002). Financial distress and the credibility of management earnings forecasts. Carnegie Mellon University.

Koch, A., Lefanowicz, C., & Shane, P. (2012). Earnings Guidance and Earnings Management Constraints. *Available at SSRN 2161762*.

Krauss, S. E. (2005). Research paradigms and meaning making: A primer. *The Qualitative Report, 10*(4), 758-770.

Krehmeyer, D., Orsagh, M., & Schacht, K. (2006). *Breaking the short-term cycle: Discussion and recommendations on how corporate leaders, asset managers, investors, and analysts can refocus on long-term value.* Paper presented at the Proceedings of the CFA Center for Financial Market

Integrity and Business Roundtable Institute for Corporate Ethics symposium series on short-termism.

Kross, W. J., Ro, B. T., & Suk, I. (2011). Consistency in meeting or beating earnings expectations and management earnings forecasts. *Journal of Accounting and Economics, 51*(1), 37-57.

Kross, W. J., & Suk, I. (2012). Does regulation FD work? evidence from analysts' reliance on public disclosure. *Journal of Accounting and Economics*.

Lambert, R. A. (2001). Contracting theory and accounting. *Journal of Accounting and Economics, 32*(1-3), 3-87.

Landry, M., & Banville, C. (1992). A disciplined methodological pluralism for MIS research. *Accounting, Management and Information Technologies, 2*(2), 77-97.

Lang, M. (1991). Time-varying stock price response to earnings induced by uncertainty about the time-series process of earnings. *Journal of Accounting research*, 229-257.

Lennox, C. S., & Park, C. W. (2006). The informativeness of earnings and management's issuance of earnings forecasts. *Journal of Accounting and Economics, 42*, 439-458.

Lev, B., & Zarowin, P. (1999). The Boundaries of Financial Reporting and How to Extend Them. *Journal of Accounting Research, 37*(2), 353-385.

Li, E., Wasley, C., & Zimmerman, J. (2010). *A Unified Framework of Management Earnings Forecasts: Voluntary, Opportunistic and Disclose or Abstain Incentives*: Working Paper. University of Rochestero. Document Number)

Li, H., Pincus, M., & Rego, S. O. (2008). Market reaction to events surrounding the Sarbanes-Oxley Act of 2002 and earnings management. *Journal of law and Economics, 51*(1), 111-134.

Li, J. Q., & Ding, Y. (2008). Institutional effects on information content of US and French management earnings forecasts: Evidence from market reactions and analyst revisions. *Advances in Accounting, incorporating Advances in International Accounting, 24* 101-109.

Libby, R., Hunton, J. E., Tan, H. U. N. T., & Seybert, N. (2008). Relationship incentives and the optimistic/pessimistic pattern in analysts' forecasts. *Journal of Accounting Research, 46*(1), 173-198.

Libby, R., & Tan, H.-T. (1999). Analysts' reactions to warnings of negative earnings surprises. *Journal of Accounting Research, 37*(2), 415-435.

Linck, J. S., Netter, J. M., & Yang, T. (2009). The effects and unintended consequences of the Sarbanes-Oxley Act on the supply and demand for directors. *Review of Financial Studies, 22*(8), 3287-3328.

Lincoln, Y. S., & Guba, E. G. (2000). The only generalization is: There is no generalization. *Case study method*, 27-44.

Liu, X. G., & Natarajan, R. (2012). The Effect of Financial Analysts' Strategic Behavior on Analysts' Forecast Dispersion. *The Accounting Review, 87*(6), 2123-2149.

Lopez, T., & Rees, L. (2002). The effect of beating and missing analysts' forecasts on the information content of unexpected earnings. . *Journal of Accounting, Auditing, and Finance, 17*, 155-184.

Matsumoto, D. A. (2002). Management's Incentives to Avoid Negative Earnings Surprises *Accounting Review, 77*(3), 483-514.

McVa, S., Nagar, V., & Tang, V. W. (2006). Trading incentives to meet the analyst forecast. Springer Science.

McVay, S., Nagar, V., & Tang, V. W. (2006). Trading incentives to meet the analyst forecast. *Review of Accounting Studies, 11*(4), 575-598.

Merchant, K. A., & Rockness, J. (1994). The ethics of managing earnings: An empirical investigation. *Journal of Accounting and Public Policy, 13*(1), 79-94.

Michaely, R., & Womack, K. L. (1999). Conflict of interest and the credibility of underwriter analyst recommendations. *Review of Financial Studies, 12*(4), 653-686.

Miller, G. S. (2002). Earnings performemance and discretionary disclosure. *Journal of Accounting Research, 40*(1), 173-204.

Myerson, R. (1979). Incentive-compatibility and the bargaining problem. *Econometrica, 47*, 61-73.

Pallant, J. (2005). *SPSS survival manual: a step by step guide to data analysis using SPSS for windows* (2 ed.). Crow Nest, N.S.W.: Allen & Unwin.

Palmrose, Z.-V., Richardson, V., & Scholz, S. (2001). Determinants of market reactions to restatement announcements.

Payne, L., & Robb, G. (2000). Earnings management: The effect of ex ante earnings expectations. *Journal of Accounting, Auditing, and Finance, 15*(4), 371.

Pinello, A. S. (2004). Individual investor reaction to the earnings expectations path and its components.

Puffer, S. M., & Weintrop, J. B. (1991). Corporate performance and CEO turnover: The role of performance expectations. *Administrative Science Quarterly, 36*, 1-19.

R. Ewert, & Waggenhofer, A. (2005). Economic effects of tightening accounting standards. *The Accounting Review, 80*(4), 1101-1124.

Rakow, K. C. (2010). The effect of management earnings forecast characteristics on cost of equity capital. *Advances in Accounting, incorporating Advances in International Accounting, 26* 37-46.

Riley, M. (2007). *Accounting Information and Analyst Forecast Errors: A study of teh Explanatory Power of Discretionary Accruals and Accruals Quality.* Texa Tech University, Texas.

Rittenberg, L. E., & Miller, P. K. (2005). Sarbanes-Oxley section 404 work: looking at the benefits. *The IIA Research Foundation, Altamonte Springs [FL].*

Rogers, J., & Van Buskirk, A. (2009). Bundled forecasts and selective disclosure of good news. *Chicago Booth Research Paper No. 09-37.*

Rogers, J. L., Skinner, D. J., & Van Buskirk, A. (2009). Earnings guidance and market uncertainty. *Journal of Accounting and Economics, 48*(1), 90-109.

Rogers, J. L., & Stocken, P. C. (2005). Credibility of Management Forecasts. *Accounting Review, 80* (4), 1233-1260.

Rogers, J. L., Van Buskirk, A., & Zechman, S. L. (2011). Disclosure tone and shareholder litigation. *The Accounting Review, 86*(6), 2155-2183.

Ronen, T., & Yaari, V. L. (2002). On The Tension Between Full Revelation And Earnings Management: A Reconsideration

Of The Revelation Principle. *Journal of Accounting, Auditing & Finance, 17*(2), 273-294.

Roychowdhury, S. (2006). Earnings management through real activities manipulation. *Journal of Accounting and Economics, 42*(3), 335-370.

Savov, S. (2006). Earnings Management, Investment, and Dividend Payments. University of Mannheim.

Shan, Y., Taylor, S., & Walter, T. (2012). Earnings Management or Measurement Error? The effect of external financing on Unexpected Accruals. University of Technology.

Shivakumar, L. (2010). Discussion of aggregate market reaction to earnings announcements. *Journal of Accounting Research, 48*(2), 335-342.

Shivakumar, L., Urcan, O., Vasvari, F. P., & Zhang, L. (2011). The debt market relevance of management earnings forecasts: Evidence from before and during the credit crisis. *Review of Accounting Studies, 16*(3), 464-486.

Sidhu, B., Smith, T., Whaley, R. E., & Willis, R. H. (2008). Regulation fair disclosure and the cost of adverse selection. *Journal of Accounting Research, 46*(3), 697-728.

Skinner, D. J. (1994). Why firms voluntarily disclose bad news. *Journal of accounting research*, 38-60.

Skinner, D. J., & Sloan, R. G. (2002). Earnings surprises, growth expectations, and stock returns or don't let an earnings torpedo sink your portfolio. *Review of Accounting Studies, 7*(2), 289-312.

Soffer, L. C., Thiagarajan, S. R., & Walther, B. R. (2000). Earningsp reannouncement strategies. *Review of Accounting Studies, 5*(1), 5-26.

Stein, J. C. (1989). Efficient capital markets, inefficient firms: a model of myopic corporate behavior. *Quarterly Journal of Economics, 104*, 655-669.

Stein, M. T. (1998). Discussion of "Bias and Accuracy of Management Earnings Forecasts: An Evaluation of the Impact of Auditing. *Contemporary Accounting Research, 15*(2), 197-201.

Stickel, S. E. (1995). The Anatomy of the Performance of Buy and Sell Recommendations. *Financial Analysts Journal, 51*(5), 25-39.

Stunda, R. A. (2008). The effects of Sarbanes-Oxley on earnings forecasts *Academy of Accounting and Financial Studies Journal*.

Su, L. N. (2005). *Earnings management and forecast guidance as mechanisms to meet or beat analysts earnings forecasts* The University of Texas, Dallas.

Sun, Y., & Xu, W. (2012). The role of accounting conservatism in management forecast bias. *Journal of Contemporary Accounting & Economics*.

Thaler, R. H. (2004). *Mental accounting matters*: Russell Sage Foundation. Princeton, NJ: Princeton University Press.

Trauth, E. M., & Jessup, L. M. (2000). Understanding computer-mediated discussions: positivist and interpretive analyses of group support system use. *Management Information Systems Quarterly, 24*(1), 43-80.

Veronesi, P. (1999). Stock market overreactions to bad news in good times: a rational expectations equilibrium model. *Review of Financial Studies, 12*(5), 975-1007.

Versano, T., & Trueman, B. (2013). Expectations Management. *Available at SSRN 2264513*.

Wang, Q. (2003). *Forecast Management: Measurement and Market Learning.* Stanford university.

Warner, J. B., Watts, R. L., & Wruck, K. H. (1988). Stock prices and top management changes. *Journal of Financial Economics, 20,* 461-492.

Watts, R., & Zimmerman, J. L. (1990). Positive Accounting Theory: A Ten Year Perspective. *The Accounting Review, 65*(1), 131-156.

Watts, R. L., & Zimmerman, J. L. (1978). Towards a positive theory of the determination of accounting standards. *The Accounting Review, 53,* 112-134.

Weisbach, M. S. (1988). Outside directors and CEO turnover. *Journal of Financial Economics, 20,* 431-460.

Williams, P. A. (1996). The relation between a prior earnings forecast by management and analyst response to a current management forecast. *Accounting Review,* 103-115.

Williamson, O. E. (1981). The economics of organization: The transaction cost approach. *American journal of sociology,* 548-577.

Xin, B. (2007). *Earnings Forecast, Earnings Management, and Asymmetric Price Response.* University of Toronto - Joseph L. Rotman School of Management.

Xu, W. (2009). Evidence that management earnings forecasts do not fully incorporate information in prior forecast errors. *Journal of Business Finance & Accounting, 36*(7-8), 822-837.

Xu, W. (2010). Do management earnings forecasts incorporate information in accruals? *Journal of Accounting and Economics, 49,* 227-246.

Yang, H. I. (2012). Capital market consequences of managers' voluntary disclosure styles. *Journal of Accounting and Economics, 53*(1–2), 167-184.

Zhu, Z. (2010). *Financial restatements: Implications for management earnings forecasts.* Unpublished Ph.D., The George Washington University, United States -- District of Columbia.

Zikmund, W. G. (2003). Sample designs and sampling procedures. *Business Research Methods, 7*, 368-400.

Zolotoy, L., Frederickson, J., & Lyon, J. (2012). Aggregate Earnings News and Stock Market Returns: The Good, the Bad and the State-Dependent. *Available at SSRN 2092087.*

_____